Cambridge English

IELTS 11

GENERAL TRAINING

WITH ANSWERS

AUTHENTIC EXAMINATION PAPERS

Cambridge University Press
www.cambridge.org/elt

Cambridge English Language Assessment
www.cambridgeenglish.org

Information on this title: www.cambridge.org/9781316503881

© Cambridge University Press and UCLES 2016

First published 2016
20 19 18 17 16 15 14 13 12 11 10 9 8 7 6 5 4 3

Printed in China by CNPIEC Beijing Congreat Printing Co., Ltd.

A catalogue record for this publication is available from the British Library

ISBN 978-1-316-61230-9 General Training Student's Book with answers with Audio China reprint edition
ISBN 978-1-316-50397-3 General Training Student's Book with answers with Audio
ISBN 978-1-316-50388-1 General Training Student's Book with answer
ISBN 978-1-316-61225-5 Academic Student's Book with answers with Audio for New Oriental School China reprint edition
ISBN 978-1-316-61223-1 Academic Student's Book with answers with Audio China reprint edition
ISBN 978-1-316-50385-0 Academic Student's Book with answers
ISBN 978-1-316-50396-6 Academic Student's Book with answers with Audio
ISBN 978-1-316-50392-8 Audio CDs (2)

Contents

Introduction

The International English Language Testing System (IELTS) is widely recognised as a reliable means of assessing the language ability of candidates who need to study or work where English is the language of communication. These Practice Tests are designed to give future IELTS candidates an idea of whether their English is at the required level.

IELTS is owned by three partners, Cambridge English Language Assessment, part of the University of Cambridge, the British Council and IDP Education Pty Limited (through its subsidiary company, IELTS Australia Pty Limited). Further information on IELTS can be found on the IELTS website www.ielts.org.

WHAT IS THE TEST FORMAT?

IELTS consists of four components. All candidates take the same Listening and Speaking tests. There is a choice of Reading and Writing tests according to whether a candidate is taking the Academic or General Training module.

Academic	General Training
For candidates wishing to study at undergraduate or postgraduate levels, and for those seeking professional registration.	For candidates wishing to migrate to an English-speaking country (Australia, Canada, New Zealand, UK), and for those wishing to train or study at below degree level.

The test components are taken in the following order:

Listening		
4 sections, 40 items approximately 30 minutes		
Academic Reading 3 sections, 40 items 60 minutes	or	**General Training Reading** 3 sections, 40 items 60 minutes
Academic Writing 2 tasks 60 minutes	or	**General Training Writing** 2 tasks 60 minutes
Speaking 11 to 14 minutes		
Total Test Time 2 hours 44 minutes		

GENERAL TRAINING TEST FORMAT

Listening

This test consists of four sections, each with ten questions. The first two sections are concerned with social needs. The first section is a conversation between two speakers and the second section is a monologue. The final two sections are concerned with situations related to educational or training contexts. The third section is a conversation between up to four people and the fourth section is a monologue.

A variety of question types is used, including: multiple choice, matching, plan/map/ diagram labelling, form completion, note completion, table completion, flow-chart completion, summary completion, sentence completion, short-answer questions.

Candidates hear the recording once only and answer the questions as they listen. Ten minutes are allowed at the end for candidates to transfer their answers to the answer sheet.

Reading

This test consists of three sections with 40 questions. The texts are taken from notices, advertisements, leaflets, newspapers, instruction manuals, books and magazines. The first section contains texts relevant to basic linguistic survival in English, with tasks mainly concerned with providing factual information. The second section focuses on the work context and involves texts of more complex language. The third section involves reading more extended texts, with a more complex structure, but with the emphasis on descriptive and instructive rather than argumentative texts.

A variety of question types is used, including: multiple choice, identifying information (True/False/Not Given), identifying the writer's views/claims (Yes/No/Not Given), matching information, matching headings, matching features, matching sentence endings, sentence completion, summary completion, note completion, table completion, flow-chart completion, diagram label completion, short-answer questions.

Writing

This test consists of two tasks. It is suggested that candidates spend about 20 minutes on Task 1, which requires them to write at least 150 words, and 40 minutes on Task 2, which requires them to write at least 250 words. Task 2 contributes twice as much as Task 1 to the Writing score.

In Task 1, candidates are asked to respond to a given situation with a letter requesting information or explaining the situation. They are assessed on their ability to engage in personal correspondence, elicit and provide general factual information, express needs, wants, likes and dislikes, express opinions, complaints, etc.

In Task 2, candidates are presented with a point of view, argument or problem. They are assessed on their ability to provide general factual information, outline a problem and present a solution, present and justify an opinion, evaluate and challenge ideas, evidence or arguments.

Candidates are also assessed on their ability to write in an appropriate style.

More information on assessing the Writing test, including Writing Assessment Criteria (public version), is available on the IELTS website.

Speaking

This test takes between 11 and 14 minutes and is conducted by a trained examiner. There are three parts:

Part 1

The candidate and the examiner introduce themselves. Candidates then answer general questions about themselves, their home/family, their job/studies, their interests and a wide range of similar familiar topic areas. This part lasts between four and five minutes.

Part 2

The candidate is given a task card with prompts and is asked to talk on a particular topic. The candidate has one minute to prepare and they can make some notes if they wish, before speaking for between one and two minutes. The examiner then asks one or two questions on the same topic.

Part 3

The examiner and the candidate engage in a discussion of more abstract issues which are thematically linked to the topic in Part 2. The discussion lasts between four and five minutes.

The Speaking test assesses whether candidates can communicate effectively in English. The assessment takes into account Fluency and Coherence, Lexical Resource, Grammatical Range and Accuracy, and Pronunciation. More information on assessing the Speaking test, including Speaking Assessment Criteria (public version), is available on the IELTS website.

HOW IS IELTS SCORED?

IELTS results are reported on a nine-band scale. In addition to the score for overall language ability, IELTS provides a score in the form of a profile for each of the four skills (Listening, Reading, Writing and Speaking). These scores are also reported on a nine-band scale. All scores are recorded on the Test Report Form along with details of the candidate's nationality, first language and date of birth. Each Overall Band Score corresponds to a descriptive statement which gives a summary of the English language ability of a candidate classified at that level. The nine bands and their descriptive statements are as follows:

9 **Expert User** – *Has fully operational command of the language: appropriate, accurate and fluent with complete understanding.*

8 **Very Good User** – *Has fully operational command of the language with only occasional unsystematic inaccuracies and inappropriacies. Misunderstandings may occur in unfamiliar situations. Handles complex detailed argumentation well.*

7 **Good User** – *Has operational command of the language, though with occasional inaccuracies, inappropriacies and misunderstandings in some situations. Generally handles complex language well and understands detailed reasoning.*

6 **Competent User** – *Has generally effective command of the language despite some inaccuracies, inappropriacies and misunderstandings. Can use and understand fairly complex language, particularly in familiar situations.*

5 **Modest User** – *Has partial command of the language, coping with overall meaning in most situations, though is likely to make many mistakes. Should be able to handle basic communication in own field.*

4 **Limited User** – *Basic competence is limited to familiar situations. Has frequent problems in understanding and expression. Is not able to use complex language.*

3 **Extremely Limited User** – *Conveys and understands only general meaning in very familiar situations. Frequent breakdowns in communication occur.*

2 **Intermittent User** – *No real communication is possible except for the most basic information using isolated words or short formulae in familiar situations and to meet immediate needs. Has great difficulty understanding spoken and written English.*

1 **Non User** – *Essentially has no ability to use the language beyond possibly a few isolated words.*

0 **Did not attempt the test** – *No assessable information provided.*

MARKING THE PRACTICE TESTS

Listening and Reading

The Answer Keys are on pages 121–128.
Each question in the Listening and Reading tests is worth one mark.

Questions which require letter / Roman numeral answers

- For questions where the answers are letters or Roman numerals, you should write *only* the number of answers required. For example, if the answer is a single letter or numeral you should write only one answer. If you have written more letters or numerals than are required, the answer must be marked wrong.

Questions which require answers in the form of words or numbers

- Answers may be written in upper or lower case.
- Words in brackets are *optional* – they are correct, but not necessary.
- Alternative answers are separated by a slash (/).
- If you are asked to write an answer using a certain number of words and/or (a) number(s), you will be penalised if you exceed this. For example, if a question specifies an answer using NO MORE THAN THREE WORDS and the correct answer is 'black leather coat', the answer 'coat of black leather' is *incorrect*.
- In questions where you are expected to complete a gap, you should only transfer the necessary missing word(s) onto the answer sheet. For example, to complete 'in the …', and the correct answer is 'morning', the answer 'in the morning' would be *incorrect*.
- All answers require correct spelling (including words in brackets).
- Both US and UK spelling are acceptable and are included in the Answer Key.
- All standard alternatives for numbers, dates and currencies are acceptable.
- All standard abbreviations are acceptable.
- You will find additional notes about individual answers in the Answer Key.

Writing

The sample answers are on pages 129–136. It is not possible for you to give yourself a mark for the Writing tasks. We have provided sample answers (written by candidates), showing their score and the examiner's comments. These sample answers will give you an insight into what is required for the Writing test.

HOW SHOULD YOU INTERPRET YOUR SCORES?

At the end of each Listening and Reading Answer Key you will find a chart which will help you assess whether, on the basis of your Practice Test results, you are ready to take the IELTS test.

In interpreting your score, there are a number of points you should bear in mind. Your performance in the real IELTS test will be reported in two ways: there will be a Band Score from 1 to 9 for each of the components and an Overall Band Score from 1 to 9, which is the average of your scores in the four components. However, institutions considering your application are advised to look at both the Overall Band Score and the Bands for each component in order to determine whether you have the language skills needed for a particular course of study. For example, if your course has a lot of reading and writing, but no lectures, listening skills might be less important and a score of 5 in Listening might be acceptable if the Overall Band Score was 7. However, for a course which has lots of lectures and spoken instructions, a score of 5 in Listening might be unacceptable even though the Overall Band Score was 7.

Once you have marked your tests, you should have some idea of whether your listening and reading skills are good enough for you to try the IELTS test. If you did well enough in one component, but not in others, you will have to decide for yourself whether you are ready to take the test.

The Practice Tests have been checked to ensure that they are of approximately the same level of difficulty as the real IELTS test. However, we cannot guarantee that your score in the Practice Tests will be reflected in the real IELTS test. The Practice Tests can only give you an idea of your possible future performance and it is ultimately up to you to make decisions based on your score.

Different institutions accept different IELTS scores for different types of courses. We have based our recommendations on the average scores which the majority of institutions accept. The institution to which you are applying may, of course, require a higher or lower score than most other institutions.

Further information

For more information about IELTS or any other Cambridge English Language Assessment examination, write to:

Cambridge English Language Assessment
1 Hills Road
Cambridge
CB1 2EU
United Kingdom

https://support.cambridgeenglish.org
http://www.ielts.org

Test 1

SECTION 1   Questions 1–10

Complete the notes below.

*Write **ONE WORD AND/OR A NUMBER** for each answer.*

HIRING A PUBLIC ROOM

Example

- the Main Hall – seats .... *200* ....

Room and cost

- the **1** .... Room – seats 100

- Cost of Main Hall for Saturday evening: **2** £ ....
  + £250 deposit (**3** .... payment is required)

- Cost includes use of tables and chairs and also **4** ....

- Additional charge for use of the kitchen: £25

Before the event

- Will need a **5** .... licence

- Need to contact caretaker (Mr Evans) in advance to arrange
  6 ....

During the event

- The building is no smoking

- The band should use the **7** .... door at the back

- Don't touch the system that controls the volume

- For microphones, contact the caretaker

After the event

- Need to know the **8** .... for the cleaning cupboard

- The **9** .... must be washed and rubbish placed in black bags

- All **10** .... must be taken down

- Chairs and tables must be piled up

SECTION 2   Questions 11–20

Questions 11–14

Complete the notes below.

Write **ONE WORD** for each answer.

Fiddy Working Heritage Farm

Advice about visiting the farm

Visitors should

- take care not to harm any **11** ....
- not touch any **12** ....
- wear **13** ....
- not bring **14** .... into the farm, with certain exceptions

---

Questions 15–20

Label the map below.

*Write the correct letter **A–I**, next to Questions 15–20.*

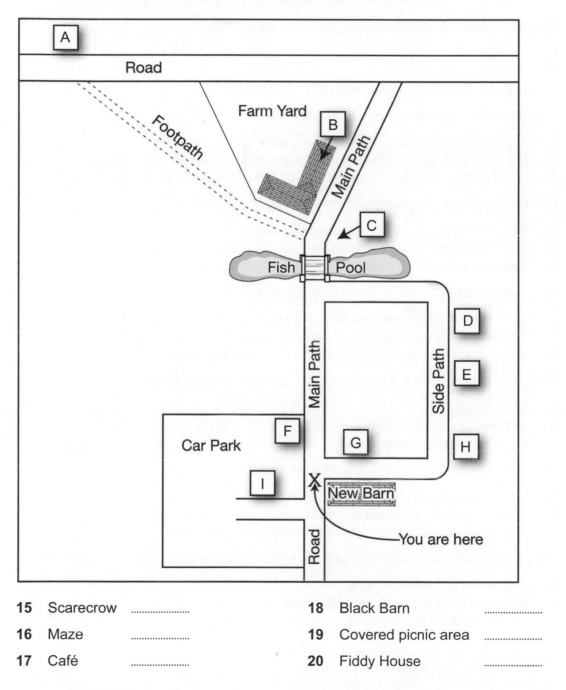

15	Scarecrow	**18**	Black Barn ....
16	Maze	**19**	Covered picnic area ....
17	Café	**20**	Fiddy House ....

SECTION 3   *Questions 21–30*

Choose the correct letter, **A**, **B** *or* **C**.

Study on Gender in Physics

21   The students in Akira Miyake's study were all majoring in

   A   physics.
   B   psychology or physics.
   C   science, technology, engineering or mathematics.

22   The aim of Miyake's study was to investigate

   A   what kind of women choose to study physics.
   B   a way of improving women's performance in physics.
   C   whether fewer women than men study physics at college.

23   The female physics students were wrong to believe that

   A   the teachers marked them in an unfair way.
   B   the male students expected them to do badly.
   C   their test results were lower than the male students'.

24   Miyake's team asked the students to write about

   A   what they enjoyed about studying physics.
   B   the successful experiences of other people.
   C   something that was important to them personally.

25   What was the aim of the writing exercise done by the subjects?

   A   to reduce stress
   B   to strengthen verbal ability
   C   to encourage logical thinking

26   What surprised the researchers about the study?

   A   how few students managed to get A grades
   B   the positive impact it had on physics results for women
   C   the difference between male and female performance

27   Greg and Lisa think Miyake's results could have been affected by

   A   the length of the writing task.
   B   the number of students who took part.
   C   the information the students were given.

28 Greg and Lisa decide that in their own project, they will compare the effects of

    A   two different writing tasks.
    B   a writing task with an oral task.
    C   two different oral tasks.

29 The main finding of Smolinsky's research was that class teamwork activities

    A   were most effective when done by all-women groups.
    B   had no effect on the performance of men or women.
    C   improved the results of men more than of women.

30 What will Lisa and Greg do next?

    A   talk to a professor
    B   observe a science class
    C   look at the science timetable

SECTION 4   *Questions 31–40*

Complete the notes below.

*Write **ONE WORD ONLY** for each answer.*

Ocean Biodiversity

Biodiversity hotspots

- areas containing many different species

- important for locating targets for **31** ....

- at first only identified on land

Boris Worm, 2005

- identified hotspots for large ocean predators, e.g. sharks

- found that ocean hotspots:

    - were not always rich in **32** ....

    - had higher temperatures at the **33** ....

    - had sufficient **34** .... in the water

Lisa Ballance, 2007

- looked for hotspots for marine **35** ....

- found these were all located where ocean currents meet

Census of Marine Life

- found new ocean species living:

    - under the **36** ....

    - near volcanoes on the ocean floor

Global Marine Species Assessment

- want to list endangered ocean species, considering:
    - population size
    - geographical distribution
    - rate of **37** ....

- Aim: to assess 20,000 species and make a distribution **38** .... for each one

Recommendations to retain ocean biodiversity

- increase the number of ocean reserves
- establish **39** .... corridors (e.g. for turtles)
- reduce fishing quotas
- catch fish only for the purpose of **40** ....

SECTION 1   *Questions 1–14*

Read the text below and answer Questions 1–5.

Is Your Child at School Today?

School Attendance Information for Parents/Carers

Introduction

Receiving a good full-time education will give your child the best possible start in life. Attending school regularly and punctually is essential if children are to make the most of the opportunities available to them. The law says that parents must ensure that their child regularly attends the school where he/she is registered.

What you can do to help

- Make sure your child arrives at school on time. This encourages habits of good timekeeping and lessens any possible classroom disruption. If your child arrives after the register has closed without a good reason, this will be recorded as an 'unauthorised' absence for that session.

- If your child has to miss school it is vital that you let the school know why, preferably on the first morning of absence. (Your child's school will have an attendance policy explaining how this should be done.)

- If you know or think that your child is having difficulties attending school you should contact the school. It is better to do this sooner rather than later, as most problems can be dealt with very quickly.

Authorised and Unauthorised Absence

If your child is absent and the school either does not receive an explanation from you, or considers the explanation unsatisfactory, it will record your child's absence as 'unauthorised', that is, as truancy.

Most absences for acceptable reasons will be authorised by your child's school:

- Sickness

- Unavoidable medical or dental appointments (if possible, arrange these for after school or during school holidays)

- An interview with a prospective employer or college

- Exceptional family circumstances, such as bereavement
- Days of religious observance.

Your child's school will not authorise absence for the following reasons:

- Shopping during school hours
- Day trips
- Holidays which have not been agreed
- Birthdays
- Looking after brothers or sisters or ill relatives.

Questions 1–5

Do the following statements agree with the information given in the text on pages 18 and 19?

In boxes 1–5 on your answer sheet, write

TRUE   *if the statement agrees with the information*
FALSE   *if the statement contradicts the information*
NOT GIVEN *if there is no information on this*

1   Children must go to the school where they are registered.

2   All arrivals after the register has closed are recorded as 'unauthorised' absences.

3   If your child is absent from school, you must send the school a letter to explain why.

4   Staff who think a child is having difficulties at school will contact the parents.

5   Schools will contact other authorities about children who take frequent unauthorised absences.

Read the text below and answer Questions 6–14.

HOLIDAY APARTMENTS TO LET

A   Sleeps 2–3. One-bedroom apartment with uninterrupted sea views. This is a small first floor apartment in a well-established apartment complex containing a range of leisure facilities and a supermarket for residents. On the edge of the town but close to cafés and restaurants. On-street parking is generally available.

B   Sleeps 2–4. Spacious one-bedroom apartment in a complex that has only just opened, five minutes' walk from the sea. Private parking in front of building. It is located in a quiet, unspoilt village with a local market, banks, cafés and restaurants. There are some fabulous championship golf courses within easy walking distance.

C   Sleeps 2+child. One-bedroom cottage (child's bed can also be provided), large terrace with uninterrupted views of the river and mountains. A truly peaceful location in a picturesque village, but less than ten minutes' drive from the coast and all the amenities of a town. Owners live nearby and are happy to help in any way they can.

D   Sleeps 2–5. Two-bedroom apartment in a complex with its own pool and beautiful views of the national park. A peaceful location just 3 km from the town centre, where there are plenty of shops and excellent sports facilities. Superb local golf courses within easy reach.

E   Sleeps 2–4. Modern one-bedroom first floor apartment in house, owners resident on ground floor. This great location offers easy access to all that this fantastic town has to offer, a few minutes' drive from its supermarket, bank, cafés, restaurants. The ferry to the island beach leaves from 100 m away. Ten minutes walk from the new shopping centre, which has many shops, food hall, cinema and multi-storey car park.

F   Sleeps 2. One-bedroom first floor apartment. Beautifully furnished, offering a high standard of comfort. Situated in a peaceful location on the edge of an inland village, with attractive views of the golf course. Many restaurants, bars, shops etc. are within easy walking distance. Garage available by arrangement with the owners.

G   Sleeps 2–4. Two-bedroom apartment in central location in busy street with shops, restaurants etc. not far from the beach. The town has ideal facilities for holidays all year round, including swimming pool, tennis courts and golf course.

Questions 6–14

The text on page 21 has seven sections, **A–G.**

For which apartment are the following statements true?

*Write the correct letter, **A–G**, in boxes 6–14 on your answer sheet.*

NB *You may use any letter more than once.*

6   It overlooks a golf course.

7   It has its own parking space.

8   It is in the centre of a town.

9   The sea can be seen from it.

10   There is a swimming pool for residents of the apartment complex.

11   It is in a new apartment complex.

12   It is part of an apartment complex with its own supermarket.

13   It has a private outdoor area where you can sit.

14   The owners will organise parking on request.

SECTION 2   *Questions 15–27*

Read the text below and answer Questions 15–21.

GZJ Travel - Recruitment Info

We're looking for keen and effective people who are passionate about travel to work as Travel Sales Consultants in our rapidly-growing team. Our recruitment process has five stages. Here's how it works:

The first stage is to use our online application form to apply for a current vacancy. This is your chance to tell us about yourself, and the qualities and experience you have that make you the ideal person for the job. For the Travel Sales Consultant role, you'll need to provide us with evidence that you have extensive experience in a marketing environment, as well as a solid academic background. If you're interested in a career as a Corporate Travel Consultant, you'll need at least one year's experience as a Travel Consultant.

If you reach Stage Two, we'll arrange a telephone discussion, where you can find out more about us, including the rewards on offer. For instance, once a year we like to acknowledge outstanding efforts and celebrate successes with our co-workers, and we have prize-giving ceremonies designed to do just this.

In Stage Three we'll be able to give you more information about GZJ Travel, and find out more about you, at an interview which you'll attend with a small group of other applicants. We'll be asking you about your ambitions and of course your sales ability, the most vital quality for our business. You'll also be required to complete a psychometric test so we can find out more about your working style and characteristics. We'll also tell you about some of the perks – for example, as a Flight Center employee you can take advantage of the free consultations conducted by our in-house health and wellbeing team, Healthwise.

Next, in Stage Four, you'll be introduced to the Area Leader and you'll also visit one of our shops, where you'll meet the team and find out more about the sort of work that's involved. If you successfully pass Stage Four, you've reached the final stage of the process and we'll be in touch with a job offer! And if you accept, we'll book you into our Learning Center to get your training under way as soon as possible. Careerwise, the department responsible for the training, will then organise individual coaching to assist in setting goals for your career path.

Questions 15–21

Complete the flow-chart below.

*Choose **NO MORE THAN THREE WORDS** from the text for each answer.*

Write your answers in boxes 15–21 on your answer sheet.

GZJ Travel – Recruitment Process

Stage One – Application form
- Go online and apply for jobs advertised
- Give proof of achievements so far both in education and in a **15** ....

(Note: additional requirements for applicants interested in the role of **16** ....)

⬇

Stage Two – Telephone discussion
- More information given about company and the **17** .... you could receive
- Information about annual event, where prizes are given to those who have made **18** ....

⬇

Stage Three – Group interview
- Chance to tell us about how good you are at selling, and also about the **19** .... you have
- Take part in a **20** .... (used to learn about your way of working)
- Information given on benefits (e.g. health consultations)

⬇

Stage Four – Individual interview
- Meet a manager, and the **21** .... working in a particular store

⬇

Stage Five – Job offer
- Job offer sent out to successful applicants

Read the text below and answer Questions 22–27.

Hilton Laboratory
Health and safety in the workplace

Personal safety

You must be familiar with the emergency procedures in your building so that you know what to do in the event of fire, spillages or other accidents. Do not enter restricted areas without authorisation, and at all times observe the warnings given. Do not wedge open fire doors or tamper with door closures, and do not block doorways, corridors or stairs, as obstructions may affect access in the event of a fire. Avoid leaving drawers and doors open unnecessarily and do not trail cables or flexes across the floor.

How to dispose of rubbish safely

We aim to protect the environment by saving and recycling glass, waste paper, and an increasing range of other materials. It is important to check materials carefully for contamination before placing them in recycling containers. Never put sharp objects such as razor blades or broken glass into waste bins without having wrapped the items carefully to protect those emptying the bins. Other waste procedures may vary – contact your Building Manager or Divisional Safety Officer for advice with regard to your particular department.

How to handle heavy objects

Make sure that shelves are not overloaded and that glass and heavy objects are stored at working height where they will be easier to reach. Use steps or ladders to reach items at height; never climb on benches, tables or chairs. Never move anything that is beyond your capability. Wherever possible you should use the trolleys provided in the workplace to do the job for you. If repetitive manual operations are routine in your work, your department will ensure you receive appropriate instruction on safe working practices and posture.

Staying alert

If you become mentally or physically tired during the working day, and find that you're feeling drowsy or not concentrating properly, you could be at risk of causing an accident or making a mistake that could harm you or your colleagues. To prevent this, make sure that you take regular breaks when necessary.

Questions 22–27

Complete the sentences below.

*Choose **NO MORE THAN TWO WORDS** from the text for each answer.*

Write your answers in boxes 22–27 on your answer sheet.

22 There are certain places in the building that staff should avoid unless they have ....

23 To ensure people can get out easily, it is important that there are no .... to exits.

24 Items which could cause injury must be .... before they are disposed of.

25 Not all departments have the same system for dealing with ...., so you need to check before throwing things away.

26 .... are available to make tasks which require moving objects easier.

27 You should have .... while you are working.

SECTION 3   *Questions 28–40*

Questions 28–34

The text on pages 28 and 29 has seven sections, **A–G**.

Choose the correct heading for each section from the list of headings below.

Write the correct number i–x, in boxes 28–34 on your answer sheet.

List of Headings

i   A decrease in the zebra population

ii   An obstruction on the traditional route

iii   An unknown species

iv   Some confusing information

v   Staying permanently in the Makgadikgadi

vi   Nearly a record in the zebra world

vii   Three different ways of living

viii The original aim of the work

ix   How was the information passed on?

x   Why it is important to study zebras

---

28   Section **A**

29   Section **B**

30   Section **C**

31   Section **D**

32   Section **E**

33   Section **F**

34   Section **G**

The Zebras' long walk across Africa

James Gifford investigates some interesting new research into migration patterns of zebras living in Botswana in southern Africa

A

For any animal to travel over 270 km in Botswana partly across the sand and low bush terrain of the Kalahari Desert is a remarkable achievement. But to do so in 11 days and without any obvious motivation, as this zebra population does, is quite extraordinary. On average their journey involves an exhausting round-trip of 588 km – between the Makgadikgadi salt pan area and the Okavango river – making it second only to the great trek undertaken by the zebra herds in the Serengeti National Park. However, what is even more incredible still in my view is that until recently it was completely unheard of.

B

Hattie Bartlam, a researcher, discovered this migration while she was tracking zebra groups, officially known as harems, by the Okavango river for her PhD. Each harem consists of a stallion and his seven or eight mares with juvenile foals. There is no loyalty between zebras beyond this social group, though harems often gather together into so-called herds. For her study, Hattie had planned to compare the small-scale movement patterns of 11 different zebra herds in the area.

C

In December, when the annual rains had transformed the roads into rivers, Hattie was, therefore, more than a little surprised when she checked the data sent by the radio collars she fits to the zebras she is tracking to find that six of the harems were 270 km away on the edge of the Makgadikgadi, a huge mineral-rich area where salt has collected over the years as water evaporates in the heat. Then, when the last of the moisture from the rains had disappeared in May the following year, five of those harems came wearily back to the Okavango. This raised the question: why, despite a plentiful supply of food and water, were the zebras being drawn eastwards to the salt pans? Even more difficult to understand was what made six of the groups travel so far, while the other five remained by the Okavango.

D

This discovery created quite a buzz in the research community. I decided to visit Hattie and she explained that a century ago the large number of Botswana's zebra and wildebeest herds and the resulting competition for grass made migration essential. One of the migration tracks went from the Okavango to Makgadikgadi. But in the late 1960s, giant fences were put up to stop foot and mouth and other diseases spreading between wildlife and domestic cattle. One of these went across the migration track. Though the animals could get round the obstacle, each leg of their journey would now be 200 km longer – an impossible distance given the lack of permanent water on the extended route. Even today, with the fence gone (it was taken down in 2004), there is dangerously little drinking water to support the zebras on the return journey to the Okavango.

E

As a zebra can live up to 20 years, the migration must have skipped at least one generation during the 40 or so years that the fences were up. This prompts another question: it has always been assumed that the young of social herbivores like zebras learn migratory behaviour from their parents, so how did the latest generation learn when and where to go? Not from their parents, who were prevented from migrating. Did they follow another species, such as elephants? We may never know.

F

Hattie's data points to the conclusion that there are several zebra populations adopting different behaviour. The first, like the vast majority of the Okavango zebras, take it easy, spending the entire year by the river. The second group, 15,000–20,000 strong, work a bit harder. They divide their time between the Makgadikgadi salt pans and the Boteti River, which is reasonably near by. They sometimes struggle to find water in the Boteti area during the dry season, often moving 30 km in search of fresh grazing. Their reward: the juicy grass around the Makgadikgadi after the rains. The final group of zebras, whose numbers are more modest (though as yet unknown), must surely be considered as among the animal kingdom's most remarkable athletes. By moving between the Okavango and the salt pans, they enjoy the best of both worlds. But the price they pay is an extraordinary journey across Botswana.

G

Endangered species naturally tend to grab the headlines, so it's refreshing for a relatively abundant animal like the zebra to be the centre of attention for once. Zebras are a vital part of the food chain: understanding their migration in turn helps us to interpret the movements of their predators, and Hattie's research has shed light on the impact of fences on migratory animals. So what triggered her interest in zebras? She explains that it is easier to get funding to study exciting animals like lions. Crucial as that undoubtedly is, she believes that herbivores like zebras are key to understanding any ecosystem. The scientific community is fortunate that people like Hattie are willing to take the hard option.

Questions 35–37

Complete the summary below.

*Choose **ONE WORD ONLY** from the text for each answer.*

Write your answers in boxes 35–37 on your answer sheet.

Social behaviour in zebras

Zebras tend to live together in small units, which experts call **35** .... Here, a male zebra has charge of a number of adult **36** .... and their young. These units sometimes assemble in bigger groupings or **37** .... , but it is still clear that the zebras' loyalty only extends to the small unit they live in.

Questions 38–40

*Choose the correct letter, **A, B, C** or **D**.*

Write the correct letter in boxes 38–40 on your answer sheet.

38 How did Hattie feel when she heard some of the zebras had travelled so far?

- **A** annoyed because she would have to follow them to Makgadikgadi
- **B** disappointed that not all of them made it back to Okavango
- **C** frustrated as the rains had made the roads unusable
- **D** unsure as to their real motivation for going

39 When describing the different Botswana zebra populations, the writer indicates

- **A** his admiration for the ones who migrate the furthest distance.
- **B** his sympathy for the ones who stay by the Okavango River.
- **C** his disbelief that those by the Boteti have difficulty finding food.
- **D** his anxiety that their migration patterns may not be able to continue.

40 What does the writer suggest in the final paragraph?

- **A** Too much time has been wasted on research into the predators like lions.
- **B** It is sometimes necessary to go against the trend in research matters.
- **C** Research will result in a ban on fences in areas where zebras live.
- **D** Research into animals which are not endangered will increase.

WRITING

WRITING TASK 1

You should spend about 20 minutes on this task.

> *You recently received a letter from a friend asking for advice about whether to go to college or to try to get a job. You think he/she should get a job.*
>
> *Write a letter to this friend. In your letter*
> * *say why he/she would not enjoy going to college*
> * *explain why getting a job is a good idea for him/her*
> * *suggest types of job that would be suitable for him/her*

Write at least 150 words.

You do **NOT** need to write any addresses.

Begin your letter as follows:

Dear .... ,

WRITING TASK 2

You should spend about 40 minutes on this task.

Write about the following topic:

> *Employers sometimes ask people applying for jobs for personal information, such as their hobbies and interests, and whether they are married or single. Some people say that this information may be relevant and useful. Others disagree.*
>
> *Discuss both these views and give your own opinion.*

Give reasons for your answer and include any relevant examples from your own knowledge or experience.

Write at least 250 words.

SPEAKING

PART 1

The examiner asks the candidate about him/herself, his/her home, work or studies and other familiar topics.

EXAMPLE

Food and cooking

*   What sorts of food do you like eating most? [Why?]
*   Who normally does the cooking in your home? [Why/Why not?]
*   Do you watch cookery programmes on TV? [Why/Why not?]
*   In general, do you prefer eating out or eating at home? [Why?]

PART 2

Describe a house/apartment that someone you know lives in.
 	
You should say:
    whose house/apartment this is
    where the house/apartment is
    what it looks like inside
and explain what you like or dislike about this person's house/apartment.

You will have to talk about the topic for one to two minutes.
You have one minute to think about what you are going to say.
You can make some notes to help you if you wish.

PART 3

Discussion topics:

Different types of home

Example questions:
What kinds of home are most popular in your country? Why is this?
What do you think are the advantages of living in a house rather than an apartment?
Do you think that everyone would like to live in a larger home? Why is that?

Finding a place to live

Example questions:
How easy is it to find a place to live in your country?
Do you think it's better to rent or to buy a place to live in? Why?
Do you agree that there is a right age for young adults to stop living with their parents? Why is that?

Test 2

SECTION 1   *Questions 1–10*

Complete the notes below.

*Write **ONE WORD AND/OR A NUMBER** for each answer.*

Enquiry about joining Youth Council

Example

Name: Roger............*Brown*.............

Age: 18

Currently staying in a **1** .... during the week

Postal address: **2** 17, ... Street, Stamford, Lincs

Postcode: **3** ....

Occupation: student and part-time job as a **4** ....

Studying **5** .... (major subject) and history (minor subject)

Hobbies: does a lot of **6** ...., and is interested in the

7 ....

On Youth Council, wants to work with young people who are
8 ....

Will come to talk to the Elections Officer next Monday at
9 .... pm

Mobile number: **10** ....

SECTION 2   *Questions 11–20*

New staff at theatre

Questions 11 and 12

*Choose **TWO** letters, **A–E**.*

Which **TWO** changes have been made so far during the refurbishment of the theatre?

A   Some rooms now have a different use.
B   A different type of seating has been installed.
C   An elevator has been installed.
D   The outside of the building has been repaired.
E   Extra seats have been added.

Questions 13 and 14

*Choose **TWO** letters, **A–E**.*

Which **TWO** facilities does the theatre currently offer to the public?

A   rooms for hire
B   backstage tours
C   hire of costumes
D   a bookshop
E   a café

Questions 15 and 16

*Choose **TWO** letters, **A–E**.*

Which **TWO** workshops does the theatre currently offer?

A   sound
B   acting
C   making puppets
D   make-up
E   lighting

Questions 17–20

Label the plan below.

*Write the correct letter, **A–G**, next to Questions 17–20.*

Ground floor plan of theatre

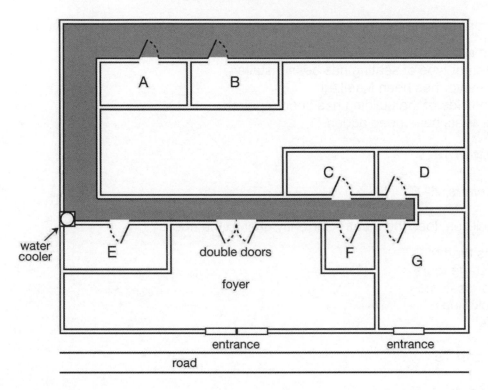

17	box office	....
18	theatre manager's office	....
19	lighting box	....
20	artistic director's office	....

SECTION 3   *Questions 21–30*

Questions 21–26

*Choose the correct letter, **A**, **B** or **C**.*

Rocky Bay field trip

21 What do the students agree should be included in their aims?

    A   factors affecting where organisms live
    B   the need to preserve endangered species
    C   techniques for classifying different organisms

22 What equipment did they forget to take on the Field Trip?

    A   string
    B   a compass
    C   a ruler

23 In Helen's procedure section, Colin suggests a change in

    A   the order in which information is given.
    B   the way the information is divided up.
    C   the amount of information provided.

24 What do they say about the method they used to measure wave speed?

    A   It provided accurate results.
    B   It was simple to carry out.
    C   It required special equipment.

25 What mistake did Helen make when first drawing the map?

    A   She chose the wrong scale.
    B   She stood in the wrong place.
    C   She did it at the wrong time.

26 What do they decide to do next with their map?

    A   scan it onto a computer
    B   check it using photographs
    C   add information from the internet

Questions 27 and 28

*Choose **TWO** letters, **A–E**.*

Which **TWO** problems affecting organisms in the splash zone are mentioned?

    A   lack of water
    B   strong winds
    C   lack of food
    D   high temperatures
    E   large waves

Questions 29 and 30

*Choose **TWO** letters, **A–E**.*

Which **TWO** reasons for possible error will they include in their report?

    A   inaccurate records of the habitat of organisms
    B   influence on behaviour of organisms by observer
    C   incorrect identification of some organisms
    D   making generalisations from a small sample
    E   missing some organisms when counting

SECTION 4   *Questions 31–40*

Complete the notes below.

*Write **ONE WORD ONLY** for each answer.*

DESIGNING A PUBLIC BUILDING:
THE TAYLOR CONCERT HALL

Introduction

The designer of a public building may need to consider the building's:

- function

- physical and **31** .... context

- symbolic meaning

Location and concept of the Concert Hall

On the site of a disused **32** ....

Beside a **33** ....

The design is based on the concept of a mystery

Building design

It's approached by a **34** .... for pedestrians

The building is the shape of a **35** ....

One exterior wall acts as a large **36** ....

In the auditorium:

• the floor is built on huge pads made of **37** ....

• the walls are made of local wood and are **38** .... in shape

• ceiling panels and **39** .... on walls allow adjustment of acoustics

Evaluation

Some critics say the **40** .... style of the building is inappropriate

READING

SECTION 1　　*Questions 1–14*

Read the text below and answer Questions 1–6.

Sustainable School Travel Strategy

Over the last 20 years, the number of children being driven to school in England has doubled. National data suggests that one in five cars on the road at 8.50 am is engaged in the school run. Children are subject to up to 3.9 times more pollution in a car that is standing in traffic than when walking or cycling to school. Reducing cars around schools makes them safer places, and walking and cycling are better for health and the environment. It has been noted by teachers that children engaging in active travel arrive at school more alert and ready to learn.

The County Council has a strong commitment to supporting and promoting sustainable school travel. We collect data annually about how pupils get to school, and our report on the Sustainable School Travel Strategy sets out in detail what we have achieved so far and what we intend to do in the future. Different parts of the County Council are working together to address the actions identified in the strategy, and we are proud that we have been able to reduce the number of cars on the daily school run by an average of 1% in each of the last three years, which is equivalent to taking approximately 175 cars off the road annually, despite an increase in pupil numbers.

All schools have a School Travel Plan, which sets out how the school and the Council can collaborate to help reduce travel to school by car and encourage the use of public transport. Contact your school to find out what they are doing as part of their School Travel Plan to help you get your child to school in a sustainable, safe way.

Questions 1–6

Do the following statements agree with the information given in the text on page 41?

In boxes 1–6 on your answer sheet, write

> **TRUE** *if the statement agrees with the information*
> **FALSE** *if the statement contradicts the information*
> **NOT GIVEN** *if there is no information on this*

1 More children are injured when walking or cycling to school than when travelling by car.

2 Children who are driven to school are more ready to learn than those who walk or cycle.

3 Every year the Council gathers information about travel to schools.

4 The Council is disappointed with the small reduction in the number of cars taking children to school.

5 The number of children in schools has risen in recent years.

6 Parents can get help with paying for their children to travel to school by public transport.

Read the text below and answer Questions 7–14.

Flu: the facts

A   Flu (influenza) is an acute viral respiratory infection. It spreads easily from person to person: at home, at school, at work, at the supermarket or on the train.

B   It gets passed on when someone who already has flu coughs or sneezes and is transmitted through the air by droplets, or it can be spread by hands infected by the virus.

C   Symptoms can include fever, chills, headache, muscle pain, extreme fatigue, a dry cough, sore throat and stuffy nose. Most people will recover within a week but flu can cause severe illness or even death in people at high risk. It is estimated that 18,500–24,800 deaths in England and Wales are attributable to influenza infections annually.

D   Vaccination is the most effective way to prevent infection. Although anyone can catch flu, certain people are at greater risk from the implications of flu, as their bodies may not be able to fight the virus. If you are over 65 years old, or suffer from asthma, diabetes, or certain other conditions, you are considered at greater risk from flu and the implications can be serious. If you fall into one of these 'at-risk' groups, are pregnant or a carer, you are eligible for a free flu vaccination.

E   If you are not eligible for a free flu vaccination, you can still protect yourself and those around you from flu by getting a flu vaccination at a local pharmacy.

F   About seven to ten days after vaccination, your body makes antibodies that help to protect you against any similar viruses that may infect you. This protection lasts about a year.

G   A flu vaccination contains inactivated, killed virus strains so it can't give you the flu. However, a flu vaccination can take up to two weeks to begin working, so it is possible to catch flu in this period.

H   A flu vaccination is designed to protect you against the most common and potent strains of flu circulating so there is a small chance you could catch a strain of flu not contained in the flu vaccine.

I   The influenza virus is constantly changing and vaccines are developed to protect against the predicted strains each year so it is important to get vaccinated against the latest strains.

Speak to your GP or nurse today to book your flu vaccination.

Questions 7–14

The text on page 43 has nine sections, **A–I**.

Which sections contain the following information?

*Write the correct letter, **A–H**, in boxes 7–14 on your answer sheet.*

NB *You may use any answer more than once.*

7   examples of people who are likely to be particularly badly affected by flu

8   how to get a vaccination if you choose to pay for it

9   why new vaccines become available

10   how long a vaccine remains effective

11   reference to the possibility of catching a different type of flu from the ones in the vaccine

12   categories of people who do not have to pay for vaccination

13   information about what a vaccine consists of

14   signs that you might have flu

SECTION 2   *Questions 15–27*

Read the text below and answer Questions 15–22.

Tips for giving an effective business presentation

Preparation

Get someone else to evaluate your performance and highlight your best skills. For example, go through your presentation in front of a colleague or relative. Think about who your audience is and what you want them to get out of the presentation. Think about content and style.

Go into the presentation room and try out any moves you may have to make, e.g. getting up from your chair and moving to the podium. Errors in the first 20 seconds can be very disorientating.

Familiarise yourself with the electronic equipment before the presentation and also have a backup plan in mind, should there be an unexpected problem like a power cut.

Dealing with presentation nervousness

A certain amount of nervousness is vital for a good presentation. The added adrenaline will keep your faculties sharp and give your presentation skills extra force. This can, however, result in tension in the upper chest. Concentrate on your breathing. Slow it right down and this will relax you. Strangely, having something to pick up and put down tends to help you do this.

It may seem an odd idea, but we seem to feel calmer when we engage in what's referred to as a displacement activity, like clicking a pen or fiddling with jewellery. A limited amount of this will not be too obvious and can make you feel more secure at the start.

Interacting with your audience

Think of your presentation as a conversation with your audience. They may not actually say anything, but make them feel consulted, questioned, challenged, then they will stay awake and attentive.

Engage with your present audience, not the one you have prepared for. Keep looking for reactions to your ideas and respond to them. If your audience doesn't appear to be following you, find another way to get your ideas across. If you don't interact, you might as well send a video recording of your presentation instead!

Structuring effective presentations

Effective presentations are full of examples. These help your listeners to see more clearly what you mean. It's quicker and more colourful. Stick to the point using three or four main ideas. For any subsidiary information that you cannot present in 20 minutes, try another medium, such as handouts.

End as if your presentation has gone well. Do this even if you feel you've presented badly. And anyway a good finish will get you some applause – and you deserve it!

Questions 15–22

Complete the sentences below.

*Choose **NO MORE THAN TWO WORDS** from the text for each answer.*

Write your answers in boxes 15–22 on your answer sheet.

15   Practising your presentation on a .... or a family member is helpful.

16   Be prepared for a problem such as a ....

17   One way to overcome pre-presentation nerves is to make your .... less rapid.

18   It is acceptable to do something called a .... at the start of the presentation to reassure you.

19   Your presentation should be like a .... with the people who have come to hear you.

20   Check constantly for .... to the points you are making.

21   Make sure you use plenty of .... to communicate your message effectively.

22   To keep the presentation short, use things like .... to provide extra details.

Read the text below and answer Questions 23–27.

How to get a job in journalism

You can get a good qualification in journalism, but what employers actually want is practical, rather than theoretical, knowledge. There's no substitute for creating real stories that have to be handed in by strict deadlines. So write for your school magazine, then maybe try your hand at editing. Once you've done that for a while, start requesting internships in newspapers in the area. These are generally short-term and unpaid, but they're definitely worthwhile, since, instead of providing you with money, they'll teach you the skills that every twenty-first century journalist has to have, like laying out articles, creating web pages, taking good digital pictures and so on.

Most reporters keep a copy of every story they've had published, from secondary school onwards. They're called cuttings, and you need them to get a job – indeed a few impressive ones can be the deciding factor in whether you're appointed or not. So start creating a portfolio now that will show off your developing talent.

It seems obvious – research is an important part of an effective job hunt. But it's surprising how many would-be journalists do little or none. If you're thorough, it can help you decide whether the job you're thinking about applying for is right for you. And nothing impresses an editor more than an applicant who knows a lot about the paper.

There are two more elements to an application – your covering letter and curriculum vitae. However, your CV is the thing that will attract an editor's attention first, so get it right. The key words are brevity, (no more than one page) accuracy (absolutely no spelling or typing errors) and clarity (it should be easy to follow).

In journalism, good writing skills are essential, so it's critical that the style of your letter is appropriate. And, make sure it conveys your love of journalism and your eagerness to do the work.

Questions 23–27

Complete the flow chart below.

*Choose **ONE WORD ONLY** from the text for each answer.*

Write your answers in boxes 23–27 on your answer sheet.

Getting a job in journalism

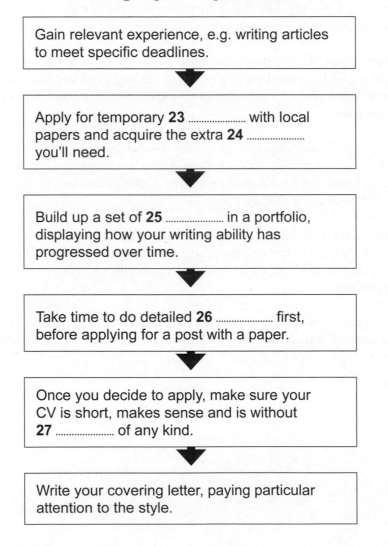

Gain relevant experience, e.g. writing articles to meet specific deadlines.

Apply for temporary **23** .... with local papers and acquire the extra **24** .... you'll need.

Build up a set of **25** .... in a portfolio, displaying how your writing ability has progressed over time.

Take time to do detailed **26** .... first, before applying for a post with a paper.

Once you decide to apply, make sure your CV is short, makes sense and is without **27** .... of any kind.

Write your covering letter, paying particular attention to the style.

SECTION 3   *Questions 28–40*

Questions 28–35

The text on pages 50 and 51 has eight sections, **A–H**.

Choose the correct heading for each section from the list of headings below.

*Write the correct number **i–x**, in boxes 28–35 on your answer sheet.*

List of Headings

i	Why Perriss chose a career in supermarkets
ii	Preparing for customers to arrive
iii	Helping staff to develop
iv	Demonstrating a different way of organising a store
v	The benefit of accurate forecasting
vi	Keeping everything running as smoothly as possible
vii	Making sure the items on sale are good enough
viii	Noticing when customers need assistance
ix	How do staff feel about Perriss?
x	Perriss's early career

---

28 Section **A**

29 Section **B**

30 Section **C**

31 Section **D**

32 Section **E**

33 Section **F**

34 Section **G**

35 Section **H**

What is it like to run a large supermarket?

Jill Insley finds out

A

You can't beat really good service. I've been shopping in the Thamesmead branch of supermarket chain Morrisons, in south-east London, and I've experienced at first hand, the store's latest maxim for improving the shopping experience – help, offer, thank. This involves identifying customers who might need help, greeting them, asking what they need, providing it, thanking them and leaving them in peace. If they don't look like they want help, they'll be left alone. But if they're standing looking lost and perplexed, a member of staff will approach them. Staff are expected to be friendly to everyone. My checkout assistant has certainly said something to amuse the woman in front of me, she's smiling as she leaves. Adrian Perriss, manager of the branch, has discussed the approach with each of his 387 staff. He says it's about recognising that someone needs help, not being a nuisance to them. When he's in another store, he's irritated by someone saying, 'Can I help you?' when he's only just walked in to have a quick look at the products.

B

How anyone can be friendly and enthusiastic when they start work at dawn beats me. The store opens at 7 am, Monday to Saturday, meaning that some staff, including Perriss, have to be here at 6 am to make sure it's clean, safe and stocked up for the morning rush. Sometimes he walks in at 6 am and thinks they're never going to be ready on time – but they always are. There's so much going on overnight – 20 people working on unloading three enormous trailers full of groceries.

C

Perriss has worked in supermarkets since 1982, when he became a trolley boy on a weekly salary of £76. 'It was less money than my previous job, but I loved it. It was different and diverse. I was doing trolleys, portering, bread, cakes, dairy and general maintenance.' After a period in the produce department, looking after the fruit and vegetables, he was made produce manager, then assistant store manager, before reaching the top job in 1998. This involved intensive training and assessment through the company's future store manager programme, learning how to analyse and prioritise sales, wastage, recruitment and many other issues. Perriss' first stop as store manager was at a store which was closed soon afterwards – though he was not to blame.

D

Despite the disappointing start, his career went from strength to strength and he was put in charge of launching new stores and heading up a 'concept' store, where the then new ideas of preparing and cooking pizzas in store, and having a proper florist, and fruit and vegetable 'markets' were trialled. All Morrisons' managers from the whole country spent three days there to see the new concept. 'That was hard work,' he says, 'long days, seven days a week, for about a year.'

E

Although he oversees a store with a large turnover, there is a strongly practical aspect to Perriss's job. As we walk around, he chats to all the staff while checking the layout of their counters and the quality of the produce. He examines the baking potato shelf and rejects three, one that has split virtually in half and two that are beginning to go green. He then pulls out a lemon that looks fine to me. When I ask why, he picks up a second lemon and says: 'Close your eyes and just feel and tell me which you would keep.' I do and realise that while one is firm and hard, the other is going a bit squashy.

F

Despite eagle-eyed Perriss pulling out fruit and veg that most of us would buy without a second thought, the wastage each week is tiny: produce worth £4,200 is marked down for a quick sale, and only £400-worth is scrapped. This, he explains, is down to Morrisons' method of ordering, still done manually rather than by computer. Department heads know exactly how much they've sold that day and how much they're likely to sell the next, based on sales records and allowing for influences such as the weather.

G

Perriss is in charge of 1,000 man-hours a week across the store. To help him, he has a key team of four, who each have direct responsibility for different departments. He is keen to hear what staff think. He recently held a 'talent' day, inviting employees interested in moving to a new job within the store to come and talk to him about why they thought they should be promoted, and discuss how to go about it. 'We had twenty-three people come through the door, people wanting to talk about progression,' he says. 'What do they need to do to become a supervisor? Twenty-three people will be better members of staff as a result of that talk.'

H

His favourite department is fish, which has a 4 m-long counter run by Debbie and Angela, who are busy having a discussion about how to cook a particular fish with a customer. But it is one of just 20 or so departments around the store and Perriss admits the pressure of making sure he knows what's happening on them all can be intense. 'You have to do so much and there could be something wrong with every single one, every day,' he says. 'You've got to minimise those things and shrink them into perspective. You've got to love the job.' And Perriss certainly does.

Questions 36–40

Do the following statements agree with the information given in the text on pages 50 and 51?

In boxes 36–40 on your answer sheet, write

> **TRUE**   *if the statement agrees with the information*
> **FALSE**   *if the statement contradicts the information*
> **NOT GIVEN**   *if there is no information on this*

36 Perriss encourages staff to offer help to all customers.

37 Perriss is sometimes worried that customers will arrive before the store is ready for them.

38 When Perriss first became a store manager, he knew the store was going to close.

39 On average, produce worth £4,200 is thrown away every week.

40 Perriss was surprised how many staff asked about promotion on the 'talent' day.

WRITING

WRITING TASK 1

You should spend about 20 minutes on this task.

You recently attended a meeting at a hotel. When you returned home, you found you had left some important papers at the hotel.

Write a letter to the manager of the hotel. In your letter

- *say where you think you left the papers*
- *explain why they are so important*
- *tell the manager what you want him/her to do*

Write at least 150 words.

You do **NOT** need to write any addresses.

Begin your letter as follows:

Dear Sir or Madam,

WRITING TASK 2

You should spend about 40 minutes on this task.

Write about the following topic:

Some people say that in all levels of education, from primary schools to universities, too much time is spent on learning facts and not enough on learning practical skills.

Do you agree or disagree?

Give reasons for your answer and include any relevant examples from your own knowledge or experience.

Write at least 250 words.

SPEAKING

PART 1

The examiner asks the candidate about him/herself, his/her home, work or studies and other familiar topics.

EXAMPLE

Friends

- How often do you go out with friends? [Why/Why not?]
- Tell me about your best friend at school.
- How friendly are you with your neighbours? [Why/Why not?]
- Which is more important to you, friends or family? [Why?]

PART 2

Describe a writer you would like to meet.

You should say:
who the writer is
what you know about this writer already
what you would like to find out about him/her
and explain why you would like to meet this writer.

You will have to talk about the topic for one to two minutes. You have one minute to think about what you are going to say. You can make some notes to help you if you wish.

PART 3

Discussion topics:

Reading and children

Example questions:
What kinds of book are most popular with children in your country? Why do you think that is?
Why do you think some children do not read books very often?
How do you think children can be encouraged to read more?

Reading for different purposes

Example questions:
Are there any occasions when reading at speed is a useful skill to have? What are they?
Are there any jobs where people need to read a lot? What are they?
Do you think that reading novels is more interesting than reading factual books? Why is that?

Test 3

SECTION 1   *Questions 1–10*

Questions 1–6

*Choose the correct letter, **A**, **B** or **C**.*

Free activities in the Burnham area

Example

The caller wants to find out about events on

A   27 June.
B   28 June.
ⓒ   29 June.

---

1   The 'Family Welcome' event in the art gallery begins at

A   10 am.
B   10.30 am.
C   2 pm.

2   The film that is now shown in the 'Family Welcome' event is about

A   sculpture.
B   painting.
C   ceramics.

3   When do most of the free concerts take place?

A   in the morning
B   at lunchtime
C   in the evening

4   Where will the 4 pm concert of Latin American music take place?

A   in a museum
B   in a theatre
C   in a library

5   The boat race begins at

A   Summer Pool.
B   Charlesworth Bridge.
C   Offord Marina.

6   One of the boat race teams

A   won a regional competition earlier this year.
B   has represented the region in a national competition.
C   has won several regional competitions.

Questions 7–10

Complete the sentences below.

*Write **ONE WORD ONLY** for each answer.*

Paxton Nature Reserve

7   Paxton is a good place for seeing rare .... all year round.

8   This is a particularly good time for seeing certain unusual ....

9   Visitors will be able to learn about .... and then collect some.

10   Part of the .... has been made suitable for swimming.

SECTION 2   *Questions 11–20*

Questions 11–15

*Choose the correct letter, **A**, **B** or **C**.*

Changes in Barford over the last 50 years

11   In Shona's opinion, why do fewer people use buses in Barford these days?

   A   The buses are old and uncomfortable.
   B   Fares have gone up too much.
   C   There are not so many bus routes.

12   What change in the road network is known to have benefited the town most?

   A   the construction of a bypass
   B   the development of cycle paths
   C   the banning of cars from certain streets

13   What is the problem affecting shopping in the town centre?

   A   lack of parking spaces
   B   lack of major retailers
   C   lack of restaurants and cafés

14   What does Shona say about medical facilities in Barford?

   A   There is no hospital.
   B   New medical practices are planned.
   C   The number of dentists is too low.

15   The largest number of people are employed in

   A   manufacturing.
   B   services.
   C   education.

Questions 16–20

What is planned for each of the following facilities?

*Choose **FIVE** answers from the box and write the correct letter, **A–G**, next to Questions 16–20.*

Plans

A   It will move to a new location.

B   It will have its opening hours extended.

C   It will be refurbished.

D   It will be used for a different purpose.

E   It will have its opening hours reduced.

F   It will have new management.

G   It will be expanded.

Facilities

16   railway station car park   ....

17   cinema   ....

18   indoor market   ....

19   library   ....

20   nature reserve   ....

SECTION 3   *Questions 21–30*

Questions 21–26

Complete the table below.

*Write **ONE WORD ONLY** for each answer.*

Subject of drawing	Change to be made
A **21** .... surrounded by trees	Add Malcolm and a **22** .... noticing him
People who are **23** .... outside the forest	Add Malcolm sitting on a tree trunk and **24** ....
Ice-skaters on **25** .... covered with ice	Add a **26** .... for each person

Questions 27–30

Who is going to write each of the following parts of the report?

*Write the correct letter, **A–D**, next to Questions 27–30.*

A	Helen only
B	Jeremy only
C	both Helen and Jeremy
D	neither Helen nor Jeremy

Parts of the report

27   how they planned the project   ....

28   how they had ideas for their stories   ....

29   an interpretation of their stories   ....

30   comments on the illustrations   ....

SECTION 4   *Questions 31–40*

Complete the notes below.

Write ONE WORD ONLY for each answer.

ETHNOGRAPHY IN BUSINESS

Ethnography: research which explores human cultures

It can be used in business:

* to investigate customer needs and **31** ....

* to help companies develop new designs

Examples of ethnographic research in business

Kitchen equipment

* Researchers found that cooks could not easily see the **32** .... in measuring cups.

Cell phones

* In Uganda, customers paid to use the cell phones of entrepreneurs.

* These customers wanted to check the **33** .... used.

Computer companies

* There was a need to develop **34** .... to improve communication between system administrators and colleagues.

Hospitals

* Nurses needed to access information about **35** .... in different parts of the hospital.

Airlines

* Respondents recorded information about their **36** .... while travelling.

Principles of ethnographic research in business

- The researcher does not start off with a hypothesis.

- Participants may be selected by criteria such as age, **37** .... or product used.

- The participants must feel **38** .... about taking part in the research.

- There is usually direct **39** .... of the participants.

- The interview is guided by the participant.

- A lot of time is needed for the **40** .... of the data.

- Researchers look for a meaningful pattern in the data.

READING

SECTION 1   *Questions 1–14*

Read the text below and answer Questions 1–6.

Summer activities at London's Kew Gardens

A   Climb up to the walkway among the trees, 18 metres above the ground, for a spectacular experience. Feel as tall as the trees and enjoy a bird's-eye view over the gardens.

B   The Nash Conservatory displays stunning images from leading wildlife photographer Heather Angel. Each photograph explores the wealth of biodiversity at Kew Gardens, from foxes to birds, tiny insects to towering trees.

C   A world of pollination comes to life in the Princess of Wales Conservatory. Find yourself in a tropical environment whilst walking through clouds of colourful butterflies as they fly around the Conservatory! Come face-to-face with gigantic sculptures of insects, birds and bats, which will help tell the fascinating stories of how they interact with plants.

D   An extraordinary sound installation created by Chris Watson. On the hour throughout the day, the Palm House is filled with the sound of the dawn and dusk choruses of birds that live in the Central and South American rainforests.

E   Come and see the fantastic outdoor exhibition of garden, wildlife and botanical photography. Walk amongst enlarged photographs and admire the wonderful garden photos – all taken by children aged 16 and under from all round the country. If you are in this age category and fancy yourself as a photographer, then you can enter for the next show!

F   Young explorers can discover the new children's outdoor play area, shaped like a plant, in Kew's magical Conservation Area. As you journey through this interactive landscape, discover the functions of every part of a plant. Tunnel through giant roots, get lost among the leaves and hide amongst the large fungi, whilst solving puzzles along the way!

G   What is biodiversity all about? Did you know that every breath we take and every move we make depends on plants? Take a guided tour to discover what biodiversity means and why it matters so much.

H   Visit our exciting and colourful exhibition of South American botanical paintings, which brings the continent's exotic and lush plants to life in works from two hundred years ago and from this century.

Questions 1–6

The text on page 63 has eight sections, **A–H**.

Which sections contain the following information?

*Write the correct letter, **A–H**, in boxes 1–6 on your answer sheet.*

1   learning what all the different sections of a plant do

2   seeing art showing plants from a different part of the world

3   the possibility of having your work exhibited

4   learning about why human beings need plants

5   something that happens daily at the same times

6   learning about the relationship between various creatures, insects and plants

Read the text below and answer Questions 7–14.

City Park and Ride

We have six purpose-built Park and Ride sites serving the city, more than almost anywhere else in the UK. Established for over 40 years, they provide around 5,000 parking spaces for cars. The sites are located on the main routes into the city centre. More than 3,000,000 passengers a year take a bus from a Park and Ride site into the city, reducing congestion and helping to improve the air quality in the city centre.

Parking at the sites is available only for those travelling from the site on a Park and Ride or other scheduled bus service, and is free. No overnight parking is permitted. Heavy goods vehicles are not permitted at the Park and Ride site at any time.

It's simple to use. Just park your car and buy your bus ticket from the bus driver, with the correct money if possible. An individual adult daily return purchased prior to 12:30 hrs for use that day costs £2.40. If purchased after 12:30 hrs it costs £2.10.

Up to four children under 16 travel free with an adult or concessionary pass holder. The return fare for unaccompanied children under 16 is £1.10.

Cycle and Ride for just £1.10 a day. Just park your cycle, motorcycle or scooter in the allocated space, and buy your ticket from the site office. You may be asked to provide evidence that you have travelled to the Park and Ride site by cycle, motorcycle or scooter.

Return tickets for concessionary bus pass holders cost £1 after 09:30 Monday to Friday and any time at weekend or bank holidays (when open). At other times there is no reduction for holders of concessionary bus passes.

Questions 7–14

Do the following statements agree with the information given in the text on page 65?

In boxes 7–14 on your answer sheet, write

> **TRUE** if the statement agrees with the information
> **FALSE** if the statement contradicts the information
> **NOT GIVEN** if there is no information on this

7 This was one of the first UK cities to introduce a Park and Ride scheme.

8 The amount of congestion in the city centre has fallen.

9 There is a special section of the car park for heavy goods vehicles.

10 Bus drivers do not give change so you must have the correct money for a ticket.

11 Ticket prices vary depending on the time of day.

12 Children under 16 travelling alone are allowed free travel.

13 The space for cycles, motorcycles and scooters is close to the site office.

14 People with concessionary bus passes must pay the full fare to travel at certain times.

SECTION 2   *Questions 15–27*

Read the text below and answer Questions 15–20.

HOW TO ORGANISE A SUCCESSFUL BUSINESS CONFERENCE

To start with

Advance planning is the key to a hassle-free conference. The key players of a successful conference are the delegates, so identify the audience and then tailor the programme you are planning to their particular needs.

Where and when

The date and venue should then be chosen. These are often interdependent, and when choosing the date take into account the timing of similar regular events which may clash. Also consider holiday periods which may mean that people are away and so will not be able to attend.

When choosing a venue, check how easy it is to reach by train and plane etc. and the availability of parking for those driving. Visit the venue personally: consider the size of the main lecture hall and whether it is big enough for the anticipated number of delegates, then look into the potential of having breakout areas for separating into a number of groups for discussions. Then check whether there is a suitable lounge area for the tea/ coffee breaks and an exhibition space for display stands if required.

Who

The next stage is to choose the speakers and invite them, making sure you give them ample notice so they are more likely to be available. Ask only those people that you know speak well. Do not try and speak yourself in addition to organising the conference, as this will be too demanding.

Contacting people

Let people know the date and venue by an early mailshot. This allows them, if they are interested, to put the date into their diaries. At the same time, contact all the speakers again, confirming their particular topic, the audio-visual aids which will be available and finding out their accommodation requirements. Ask them to provide a written summary of their presentation for distribution to delegates at the conference.

Final arrangements

Approximately 4–5 weeks before the conference, confirm the provisional numbers with the venue. Contact them again about two weeks prior to the conference to confirm final numbers, decide on menus and finalise the arrangements.

Prepare delegate packs to include a name badge, delegate list and programme. The venue should provide pads of paper and pens. Then prepare questionnaires for all delegates to complete at the end of the conference. Their responses will enable you to gauge the success of the conference and start planning the next one!

Questions 15–20

Complete the notes below.

Choose **ONE WORD ONLY** from the text for each answer.

Write your answers in boxes 15–20 on your answer sheet.

ORGANISING A BUSINESS CONFERENCE

First steps:

- decide who the conference is for

- ensure the programme fulfils delegates' requirements

Venue and timing:

- try to avoid scheduling the conference during **15** .... times or when other annual conferences occur

- check accessibility by different modes of transport

- choose a place with a large hall and also **16** .... spaces for smaller meetings

Speakers:

- choose appropriate speakers

- give the speakers as much **17** .... as possible

Communication:

- send out a mailshot to potential delegates

- confirm individual details with speakers, check if they will need accommodation and request a **18** .... of their presentation

Final tasks:

- give the venue precise numbers of attendees

- make sure each person attending receives information about the conference and a **19** .... for identification

- use **20** .... to get opinions on the conference

---

Read the text below and answer Questions 21–27.

How to deal with the annual performance appraisal

The annual performance appraisal can help improve your productivity and provide a foundation for your work priorities. It is, however, critical to have the right attitude and approach. Knowing what areas your superiors see as your weaknesses is the most direct way of increasing the likelihood of being considered for promotion, if that is what you are looking for.

Preparation

Send your boss a summary of your achievements. Reminding your boss of activities, special assignments you did, and projects you were in charge of helps him or her create a more accurate performance appraisal. Consider keeping notes of these on a regular basis to make it easier to provide the data when required.

Create a list of questions you would like to discuss during your appraisal. This one-on-one time with your boss is an excellent opportunity to ask him or her about your role in the company, request any additional responsibilities you would like and clarify your priorities. But it is best to focus your attention around personal and professional improvements, rather than financial considerations, such as an increase in salary.

During the appraisal

Present a positive attitude as soon as you enter the appraisal room. This approach may lead to a more constructive discussion of review items. Avoid taking any negative assessments that are offered as a personal attack, but rather try to take them on board calmly, because if you put the failings right you will improve your performance. A realistic assessment of your strengths and weaknesses can be one of the most beneficial ways of helping you advance in the company.

After the appraisal

Create a list of personal goals based on your performance appraisal. Make the items detailed and measurable if possible. Send this list to your boss so he or she knows you took the appraisal seriously. Use this list to help achieve higher scores on your next performance appraisal. Six months after the appraisal, ask for a mid-term review with your boss to discuss your progress. This session should be more relaxed and informal than the official review. Ask for more feedback to help you improve. Checking in with your boss helps him or her remember your dedication as far as your job is concerned, and may help remove any criticisms before they become a review point on your next formal appraisal.

Questions 21–27

Complete the sentences below.

*Choose **ONE WORD ONLY** from the text for each answer.*

Write your answers in boxes 21–27 on your answer sheet.

21 By learning at an appraisal what areas of work need improving, staff can improve their chances of getting ....

22 It is important to think of some .... that can be used during the appraisal.

23 The appraisal can be a good time to ask the boss for extra ....

24 React .... to any criticism.

25 It is helpful to identify a number of individual .... arising from the appraisal comments.

26 Staff can request a meeting half-way through the year to look at the .... which has been achieved.

27 If staff act on any appraisal comments, they will demonstrate their .... to their work.

SECTION 3   *Questions 28–40*

Questions 28–33

The text on pages 72 and 73 has six sections, **A–F**.

Choose the correct heading for each section from the list of headings below.

*Write the correct number, **i–viii**, in boxes 28–33 on your answer sheet.*

List of Headings

i   Gaining public recognition

ii   Reasons for continuing to make the long journey

iii   A disappointment followed by desirable outcomes

iv   The main stages of the plan

v   A growth in the number of natural predators

vi   Increasing threats

vii   A very unusual feature of these birds

viii Cautious optimism

28   Section **A**

29   Section **B**

30   Section **C**

31   Scction **D**

32   Section **E**

33   Section **F**

Efforts to save a special bird – the spoon-billed sandpiper

Last year an international team of ornithologists devised a bold
plan to rescue one of the world's rarest birds. Gerrit Vyn reports.

A   At first glance the spoon-billed sandpiper resembles other small migratory birds of the sandpiper family that breed across the Arctic. But it is the only one to have developed a flattened bill that flares out into a 'spoon' at the end, and that makes it special. If it becomes extinct, thousands of years of evolution will come to an end, which would be a real tragedy.

The bird's Russian name, kulik-lopaten, means 'shovel beak', which is an apt description of a remarkable structure. The bill is 19 mm long and 10 mm wide near the tip and the edges are lined with sharp serrations, called papillae. Theories have varied as to how the bill functions; one suggestion is that the sandpiper sweeps it through the water in a similar fashion to its larger namesake, the spoonbill. But Nigel Clark, a leading authority on the sandpiper, says the comparison is misleading.

B   Until a few years ago, the spoon-billed sandpiper had never been fully documented, which added to its fascination. But an air of mystery is not helpful if you're a Critically Endangered species. So the organisation 'Birds Russia' decided to produce a photographic and audio record of this imperilled bird with the help of experts round the world. In May of last year, I joined the international expedition to one of the species' last breeding strongholds in North-East Russia. The primary aim of the two-and-a-half month expedition, however, was to collect eggs from wild sandpipers; those eggs would then be hatched in captivity nearby. Later, the chicks would be flown to the Wildfowl and Wetlands Trust (WWT) headquarters at Slimbridge in the UK, in order to establish a small, self-sustaining population there. These birds would provide a 'safety net', an insurance policy against the wild birds dying out.

C   You might wonder why birds like the spoon-billed sandpiper travel such great distances, about 8,000 km in total, from their wintering grounds on the tropical coasts of Bangladesh, Burma and Vietnam in South-East Asia to breed on the low land, commonly called tundra, in North-East Russia, but from the birds' point of view it is worth it. Though they often arrive to find hostile, wintry weather while they are finding their mates and making their nests, there are relatively few predators there, and the abundance of insects that emerge during the brief but intense Arctic summer creates ideal conditions for raising their chicks.

D   Two main factors are responsible for the sandpiper's recent rapid decline: the ongoing destruction of stopover habitat on its migration route and hunting on its wintering grounds. The development of new industrial cities is destroying former tidal areas, where sandpipers and other migratory birds used to rest and refuel. Subsistence hunting is certainly a hazard in some Asian countries, where hunters trap birds for food. Conservationists are targeting this problem with small-scale interventions. For example, hunters from 40 villages have been given alternative sources of income, such as cool boxes in which they can take fish to sell at markets, in return for a halt to the bird-netting.

E   Once the expedition team had reached its destination, it was seven days before we spotted the first sandpiper. In the following days, more began to arrive and the males' song was heard, advertising their patches of territory to potential mates. As the sandpipers paired up, the song gave way to the quiet of egg-laying and incubation. In total nine nests were found. The first one was lost to a predator, along with the female attending it. This was a stark reminder of the vulnerability of a tiny population to natural events, such as storms or predation.

The team then selected donor nests and transferred the eggs to specially prepared incubators. They collected 20 eggs in all, taking entire clutches each time – it was early in the breeding season, so the females were likely to lay replacements. Then 50 days after our arrival, the moment arrived: I witnessed my first wild spoon-billed sandpipers hatch. I had been lying inside a wind-battered hide for 36 hours when I saw the first tiny chicks emerge from the eggs. Having hidden a microphone near the nest, I could also just hear their first calls. Later, I watched them stumbling through the 15 cm-high jungle of grasses on comically oversized legs and feet. But my joy was tempered by concern. Difficulties on their migration route and in their wintering areas meant that other tiny creatures like these faced immense dangers.

F   The complex rescue plan does give some grounds for hope. Young chicks were flown to WWT Slimbridge last year and again this summer. A high-tech biosecure unit has been built for them there. It is divided in two, with the older birds in one section and this year's chicks in the other. To minimise the risk of infections, staff change into full-body overalls and rubber shoes and wash their hands before entering. Hygiene is crucial: even a single strand of human hair could harm the chicks by becoming twisted round their legs or bills. The rescue plan's final stage, once the captive flock has built up sufficiently, will be to fly eggs back to Russia, to release the chicks there. It's a gamble, but when the survival of a species this special is at stake, you have to try.

Questions 34–37

*Choose the correct letter, **A**, **B**, **C** or **D**.*

Write the correct letter in boxes 34–37 on your answer sheet.

34 What was the main purpose of the international expedition?

    A to add sandpiper eggs to an international frozen egg bank
    B to maintain a small group of sandpipers for future generations
    C to make an audiovisual record of the Russian sandpiper colony
    D to protect a colony of wild sandpipers through a breeding season

35 What do we learn about the drop in the sandpiper population?

    A The birds are increasingly being hunted on their way north to Russia.
    B Scientists are managing to reduce deaths from netting considerably.
    C Efforts are being made to protect some of their coastal habitat sites.
    D Economic growth is one of the underlying causes of the decline.

36 Which feeling did the writer express when the sandpiper chicks hatched?

    A relief that his long wait was over
    B surprise at the sound of their song
    C worry about birds of the same species
    D amazement that they could walk so soon

37 The writer describes the sandpipers' unit at WWT Slimbridge to emphasise

    A how much care is being devoted to their welfare.
    B how much money is being spent on the project.
    C his surprise at how fragile the young birds are.
    D his confidence in the technology available.

Questions 38–40

Complete the summary below.

Choose **ONE WORD ONLY** *from the text for each answer.*

Write your answers in boxes 38–40 on your answer sheet.

The life cycle of the spoon-billed sandpiper

In early spring, spoon-billed sandpipers return to their breeding grounds in Russia in the area known as **38** .... Although the weather there is often very harsh to begin with, there are obvious advantages to the sandpipers. There is above all a plentiful supply of **39** .... , and this makes it possible for the sandpiper chicks to develop well. The lack of **40** .... is another definite advantage. As a result, a good proportion of the chicks grow up to face the long flight to the South-East Asian coasts.

WRITING

WRITING TASK 1

You should spend about 20 minutes on this task.

> *Your local council is considering closing a sports and leisure centre that it runs, in order to save money.*
>
> *Write a letter to the local council. In your letter*
> - *give details of how you and your friends or family use the centre*
> - *explain why the sports and leisure centre is important for the local community*
> - *describe the possible effects on local people if the centre closes*

Write at least 150 words.

You do **NOT** need to write any addresses.

Begin your letter as follows:

Dear Sir or Madam,

WRITING TASK 2

You should spend about 40 minutes on this task.

Write about the following topic:

> *News stories on TV and in newspapers are very often accompanied by pictures.*
>
> *Some people say that these pictures are more effective than words.*
>
> *What is your opinion about this?*

Give reasons for your answer and include any relevant examples from your own knowledge or experience.

Write at least 250 words.

SPEAKING

PART 1

The examiner asks the candidate about him/herself, his/her home, work or studies and other familiar topics.

EXAMPLE

Photographs

- What type of photos do you like taking? [Why/Why not?]
- What do you do with photos you take? [Why/Why not?]
- When you visit other places, do you take photos or buy postcards? [Why/Why not?]
- Do you like people taking photos of you? [Why/Why not?]

PART 2

Describe a day when you thought the weather was perfect.

You should say:
where you were on this day
what the weather was like on this day
what you did during the day
and explain why you thought the weather was perfect on this day.

You will have to talk about the topic for one to two minutes. You have one minute to think about what you are going to say. You can make some notes to help you if you wish.

PART 3

Discussion topics:

Types of weather

Example questions:
What types of weather do people in your country dislike most? Why is that?
What jobs can be affected by different weather conditions? Why?
Are there any important festivals in your country that celebrate a season or type of weather?

Weather forecasts

Example questions:
How important do you think it is for everyone to check what the next day's weather will be? Why?
What is the best way to get accurate information about the weather?
How easy or difficult is it to predict the weather in your country? Why is that?

Test 4

SECTION 1   Questions 1–10

Questions 1–7

Complete the table below.

Write ONE WORD AND/OR A NUMBER for each answer

Event	Cost	Venue	Notes
Jazz band	*Example* Tickets available for £ ......15......	The **1** .... school	Also appearing: Carolyn Hart (plays the **2** ....)
Duck races	£1 per duck	Start behind the **3**	Prize: tickets for **4** .... held at the end of the festival. Ducks can be bought in the **5** ....
Flower show	Free	**6** .... Hall	Prizes presented at 5 pm by a well-known **7** ....

Questions 8–10

Who is each play suitable for?

*Write the correct letter, **A**, **B** or **C**, next to Questions 8–10.*

A	mainly for children
B	mainly for adults
C	suitable for people of all ages

Plays

8   The Mystery of Muldoon   ....

9   Fire and Flood   ....

10   Silly Sailor   ....

SECTION 2   *Questions 11–20*

Questions 11–16

What does the speaker say about each of the following collections?

*Choose **SIX** answers from the box and write the correct letter, **A–G**, next to Questions 11–16.*

Comments
A   was given by one person
B   was recently publicised in the media
C   includes some items given by members of the public
D   includes some items given by the artists
E   includes the most popular exhibits in the museum
F   is the largest of its kind in the country
G   has had some of its contents relocated

Collections

11 20th- and 21st-century paintings ....

12 19th-century paintings   ....

13 Sculptures   ....

14 'Around the world' exhibition   ....

15 Coins   ....

16 Porcelain and glass   ....

Questions 17–20

Label the plan below.

*Write the correct letter, **A–H**, next to Questions 17–20.*

Basement of museum

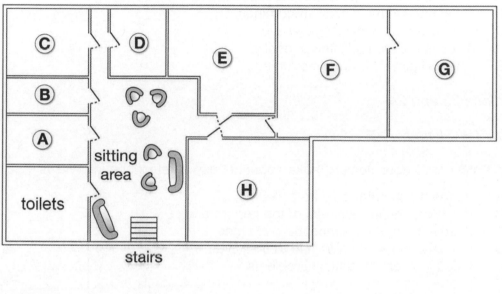

17 restaurant   ....

18 café   ....

19 baby-changing facilities ....

20 cloakroom   ....

SECTION 3   *Questions 21–30*

Questions 21 and 22

*Choose **TWO** letters, **A–E**.*

Which **TWO** characteristics were shared by the subjects of Joanna's psychology study?

    A   They had all won prizes for their music.
    B   They had all made music recordings.
    C   They were all under 27 years old.
    D   They had all toured internationally.
    E   They all played a string instrument.

Questions 23 and 24

*Choose **TWO** letters, **A–E**.*

Which **TWO** points does Joanna make about her use of telephone interviews?

    A   It meant rich data could be collected.
    B   It allowed the involvement of top performers.
    C   It led to a stressful atmosphere at times.
    D   It meant interview times had to be limited.
    E   It caused some technical problems.

Questions 25 and 26

*Choose **TWO** letters, **A–E**.*

Which **TWO** topics did Joanna originally intend to investigate in her research?

    A   regulations concerning concert dress
    B   audience reactions to the dress of performers
    C   changes in performer attitudes to concert dress
    D   how choice of dress relates to performer roles
    E   links between musical instrument and dress choice

Questions 27–30

*Choose the correct letter, **A**, **B** or **C**.*

27 Joanna concentrated on women performers because

    A   women are more influenced by fashion.
    B   women's dress has led to more controversy.
    C   women's code of dress is less strict than men's.

28 Mike Frost's article suggests that in popular music, women's dress is affected by

    A   their wish to be taken seriously.
    B   their tendency to copy each other.
    C   their reaction to the masculine nature of the music.

29 What did Joanna's subjects say about the audience at a performance?

    A   The musicians' choice of clothing is linked to respect for the audience.
    B   The clothing should not distract the audience from the music.
    C   The audience should make the effort to dress appropriately.

30 According to the speakers, musicians could learn from sports scientists about
    A   the importance of clothing for physical freedom.
    B   the part played by clothing in improving performance.
    C   the way clothing may protect against physical injury.

SECTION 4   *Questions 31–40*

Complete the notes below.

Write **ONE WORD ONLY** for each answer.

The use of soil to reduce carbon dioxide (CO_2) in the atmosphere

Rattan Lal:

* Claims that 13% of CO_2 in the atmosphere could be absorbed by agricultural soils
* Erosion is more likely in soil that is **31** ....
* Lal found soil in Africa that was very **32** ....
* It was suggested that carbon from soil was entering the atmosphere

Soil and carbon:

* plants turn CO_2 from the air into carbon-based substances such as **33** ....
* some CO_2 moves from the **34** .... of plants to microbes in the soil
* carbon was lost from the soil when agriculture was invented

Regenerative agriculture:

* uses established practices to make sure soil remains fertile and **35** ....
* e.g. through year-round planting and increasing the **36** .... of plants that are grown

California study:

* taking place on a big **37** .... farm
* uses compost made from waste from agriculture and **38** ....

Australia study:

* aims to increase soil carbon by using **39** .... that are always green

Future developments may include:

* reducing the amount of fertilizer used in farming
* giving farmers **40** .... for carbon storage, as well as their produce

READING

SECTION 1   *Questions 1–14*

Read the text below and answer Questions 1–7.

Visitor attractions in southern England

A   Blackthorn Castle

This famous, historically accurate, reconstructed castle and village enables visitors to travel back in time. Explore the grounds and experience the atmosphere of an ancient lifestyle. In the fields you can see the type of sheep that the original inhabitants of the castle probably kept. Homemade snacks are on sale.

B   Withney Wetland Centre

Visitors will enjoy a visit to Withney whatever the season. In winter, for example, they can watch from the centrally heated observatory as thousands of swans feed on the water. Trained wardens give informative talks or lead guided walks round the site. The visitors' centre may also be hired for private or corporate events.

C   Headley Hall

Headley Hall is a large seventeenth-century country house, preserved as it was when it was built. Take time to admire the various works of art displayed, and visit the huge kitchen complete with period equipment – demonstrations are given at weekends. In the park there is space for the younger visitors to run around, and picnic tables are available.

D   Lewis House

Lewis House is the birthplace of Frank Lewis, a renowned painter of the eighteenth century. More of his works are on display here than anywhere else in the world. Visitors can see Lewis's studio and some of the articles he used on a daily basis.

E   Canford Wildlife Centre

At Canford we have a new walk-through exhibit called Island Magic. Here visitors can observe many species from the tropical island of Madagascar and read about some of the urgent conservation projects that are taking place there to save endangered species from extinction.

F   Oakwell Museum

This is an ideal venue for families. They can visit the childhood gallery with its large playroom, and listen to stories told by actors dressed in the costumes of a hundred years ago. They can also enjoy the popular games and wooden animals of that period.

Questions 1–7

*Look at the six visitor attractions in southern England, **A–F**, on pages 85 and 86.*

For which visitor attraction are the following statements true?

*Write the correct letter, **A–F**, in boxes **1–7** on your answer sheet.*

NB *You may use any letter more than once.*

1   Visitors can look at animals from another part of the world.

2   People can hold a business conference in this place.

3   Visitors can find out what toys were used in the last century.

4   Activities are available all year round here.

5   You can buy light meals here.

6   Visitors can see how food was prepared in the past.

7   You can visit modern imitations of old buildings here.

Read the text below and answer Questions 8–14.

Paragliding in Australia

What is paragliding?

Paragliding is a kind of flying, but instead of the wing being made of metal, wood or plastic, it is made of nylon or polyester. The wing (known as a canopy) is attached to a harness by lines, not dissimilar to a parachute. The harness is where the pilots sit – and they report that it outperforms a parachute in terms of comfort.

Is it safe?

Like sailing and deep-sea diving, paragliding is as safe as the person doing it. The big advantage is that it's probably the slowest form of aviation, so if you do crash you'll hit the ground quite gently!

Where do I learn?

There are lots of schools, mainly based inland by appropriate hills or mountains, and there are also schools on the coast near spectacular cliffs. These are very attractive, though the prospect of landing in the sea seems to dissuade beginners! All schools will show you within a couple of days how to inflate the canopy, launch and land. They use radio instruction, tandem flying practice and schoolroom theory sessions to help you get the most from paragliding. It takes about seven days to get your basic licence; then you're free to fly independently at sites across Australia.

What do I need?

Pilots normally wear warm clothes, in case they get very high up, and a helmet in case they stumble on landing. In terms of gear, schools supply basic training, canopies, harnesses, etc. However, you'll probably want to buy your own more sophisticated equipment, which you'll be able to choose much better once you've tried some out on your course.

Who can do it?

There's no upper age limit provided your instructor deems you capable, but the youngest anybody can paraglide is 14. Anybody with good eyesight and good balance is a potential paraglider pilot. It's a very relaxed sport as you're mostly sitting down. You'll probably experience pain in some muscles you didn't know you had whilst learning, but many of those will be due to the walk up the training hill to launch. Flying a paraglider is a great sport. We hope to see you in the air with us this season!

Questions 8–14

Do the following statements agree with the information given in the text on page 88?

In boxes 8–14 on your answer sheet, write

> **TRUE**   *if the statement agrees with the information*
> **FALSE**   *if the statement contradicts the information*
> **NOT GIVEN** *if there is no information on this*

8   A paraglider is more comfortable than a parachute.

9   Most paragliding schools are situated by the sea.

10   Learners must pass a theory test in order to get their licence.

11   Learners are able to paraglide unaccompanied after a week's course.

12   It is advisable to purchase some equipment before you do your training.

13   Fit people of any age can take up paragliding.

14   The preliminary uphill walk may strain some of your muscles.

SECTION 2   *Questions 15–27*

Read the text below and answer Questions 15–21.

How to prepare for an interview

Why prepare?

There are three main reasons.

One: Although you can't guess every question you might be asked, if you are prepared you can tailor your answers to fit.

Two: If you're well prepared, you will have more confidence and this will affect the way you come across.

Three: Attitude matters. Prospective employers will choose a not-quite-perfect but willing candidate over a brilliant one who obviously isn't bothered.

What to prepare?

Find out about the organisation

*   Visit the website and read any materials that you have been sent. If nothing has been sent, phone the company to ask for any reading matter they may have.

*   Talk to anyone you know who works there already.

Find out about the job

*   Ask for a job description or specification. This will tell you the duties that go with the job.

*   Talk to anyone you know who is familiar with the work you may be doing.

Find out what the employer is looking for

*   Make a list of the skills specified in the job advertisement.

*   Think of examples to back up claims that you have these skills.

You can then answer most of the questions that will come up, such as 'Tell me more about how you work in a team'.

Add in a few 'lessons learned' – what you did and how you might have done it better. You can also outline any voluntary work you have done for a charity, or any experience of paid work in an unrelated sector.

Preparing for other kinds of questions

Interviewers are also looking for someone who is likely to stay with the organisation and progress within it. Prepare to answer questions about your ambitions for the future.

You may also be asked to account for gaps in your career history, if you have any. Be positive and accentuate the learning or experience you gained during these periods.

Preparing your own questions

*   **Do** ask technical questions about software, systems and structures and how things are done.

*   **Do** ask about possibilities for training.

*   **Don't** ask about salary unless you have been offered the job.

When you've prepared as much as this, you've got a good chance of success.

Good luck!

Questions 15–21

Complete the sentences below.

*Choose **ONE WORD ONLY** from the text for each answer.*

Write your answers in boxes 15–21 on your answer sheet.

15 By preparing for your interview, you will gain .... which will help you present yourself well.

16 Read through any documents you have received about the company and also go to their ....

17 Check the job description to find out what .... are involved in the post you have applied for.

18 Interviewers may be interested to hear about any unpaid help you have given to a ....

19 Be ready to talk about your .... for the development of your career.

20 Explain any .... that there are in your work record and clarify how you used the time to improve your skills.

21 Questions about .... should be delayed until a later stage.

Read the text below and answer Questions 22–27.

Setting up your own business

Here are some ideas about how you should start:

Know your market

So you know what you want to sell – the most important thing is that it should be something that people want to buy. Start by thinking about who your target customers are. Are they people who live locally? Are they a particular group of people?

Now look at your competitors. What is different about what you will be doing and how will you persuade people to come to you instead of going to someone who is already established?

How will you reach the customers?

Will you promote your product by phoning people, or visiting local traders, or advertising in magazines or online? Will your delivery system be direct or through shops?

How will your business work?

Now think about what your business needs to succeed. Do you need to look for premises or can you work from home? Do you need to invest in manufacturing equipment to start with?

Is the business something that you can do on your own, or if you get more work will you be looking to recruit staff? If so, what skills would they need?

Whether you're a sole operator or are looking to recruit a team, effective management is essential.

The law regulates how companies are run and you need to set aside the time to see that this is done properly, in relation to issues like accounting, insurance and tax.

The money!

As you are working out the prices for your products, you need to make sure you build in all your costs. Remember you will probably need help from an accountant at least once a year, so build that in too, and do a forecast of how much money you think will flow in and out of the business.

Look at what you expect to happen over the next three years – and work out what you need to do to break even, as well as the turnover that you hope to achieve to give you a profit. If you think you will need to find some funding to help get the business off the ground, how much will you need and who will you approach to get it?

Your business plan

Now write it all up and call it a business plan.

Questions 22–27

Complete the sentences below.

*Choose **ONE WORD ONLY** from the text for each answer.*

Write your answers in boxes 22–27 on your answer sheet.

Step 1:

Decide who you are going to sell to and compare yourself with the **22** .... you are going to have.

Step 2:

Consider how you will market your product and your method of **23** ....

Step 3:

Decide if you will have to find **24** .... to work in, or buy equipment.

Step 4:

Think whether you will need to take on staff as your business grows.

Step 5:

Make sure you deal with the accounts and other essentials in accordance with the **25** ....

Step 6:

Calculate all the **26** .... involved in your business when deciding how much to charge.

Step 7:

Calculate the turnover you are aiming for in order to make a profit in the first three years.

Step 8:

Consider if you require any **27** .... to start your business, and where to find it.

SECTION 3   *Questions 28–40*

Questions 28–33

The text on pages 95 and 96 has six sections, **A–F**.

Choose the correct heading for each section from the list of headings below.

*Write the correct number, **i–ix**, in boxes 28–33 on your answer sheet.*

List of Headings

i   The need for population reduction

ii   The problem with being a fussy eater

iii Reproductive patterns

iv   The need for further research

v   A possible solution to falling numbers

vi   The fastest runners

vii A rather lonely beginning

viii A comparison between past and present survival rates

ix   Useful physical features

---

28   Paragraph **A**

29   Paragraph **B**

30   Paragraph **C**

31   Paragraph **D**

32   Paragraph **E**

33   Paragraph **F**

Understanding hares

With its wild stare, swift speed and secretive nature, the UK's brown hare is the rabbit's mysterious cousin. Even in these days of agricultural intensification, the hare is still to be seen in open countryside, but its numbers are falling.

A   Like many herbivores, brown hares spend a relatively large amount of their time feeding. They prefer to do this in the dark, but when nights are short, their activities do spill into daylight hours. Wherever they live, hares appear to have a fondness for fields with a variety of vegetation, for example short as well as longer clumps of grasses. Studies have demonstrated that they benefit from uncultivated land and other unploughed areas on farms, such as field margins. Therefore, if farmers provided patches of woodland in areas of pasture as well as assorted crops in arable areas, there would be year-round shelter and food, and this could be the key to turning round the current decline in hare populations.

B   Brown hares have a number of physical adaptations that enable them to survive in open countryside. They have exceptionally large ears that move independently, so that a range of sounds can be pinpointed accurately. Positioned high up on their heads, the hares' large golden eyes give them 360° vision, making it hard to take a hare by surprise. Compared to mammals of a similar size, hares have a greatly enlarged heart and a higher volume of blood in their bodies, and this allows for superior speed and stamina. In addition, their legs are longer than those of a rabbit, enabling hares to run more like a dog and reach speeds of up to 70 kph.

C   Brown hares have unusual lifestyles for their large size, breeding from a young age and producing many leverets (babies). There are about three litters of up to four leverets every year. Both males and females are able to breed at about seven months old, but they have to be quick because they seldom live for more than two years. The breeding season runs from January to October, and by late February most females are pregnant or giving birth to their first litter of the year. So it seems strange, therefore, that it is in March, when the breeding season is already underway, that hares seemingly go mad: boxing, dancing, running and fighting. This has given rise to the age-old reference to 'mad March hares'. In fact, boxing occurs throughout the breeding season, but people tend to see this behaviour more often in March. This is because in the succeeding months, dusk – the time when hares are most active – is later, when fewer people are about. Crops and vegetation are also taller, hiding the hares from view. Though it is often thought that they are males fighting over females, boxing hares are usually females fighting off males. Hares are mostly solitary, but a female fights off a series of males until she is ready to mate. This occurs several times through the breeding season because, as soon as the female has given birth, she will be ready to mate again.

D   But how can females manage to do this while simultaneously feeding themselves and rearing their young? The reason is that hares have evolved such self-sufficient young. Unlike baby rabbits, leverets are born furry and mobile. They weigh about 100 g at birth and are immediately left to their own devices by their mothers. A few days later, the members of the litter creep away to create their own individual resting places, known as 'forms'. Incredibly, their mother visits them only once every 24 hours and, even then, she only suckles them for a maximum of five minutes each. This lack of family contact may seem harsh to us, but it is a strategy that draws less attention from predators. At the tender age of two weeks, leverets start to feed themselves, while still drinking their mother's milk. They grow swiftly and are fully weaned at four weeks, reaching adult weight at about six months.

E   Research has shown that hares' milk is extremely rich and fatty, so a little goes a long way. In order to produce such nutritious milk, females need a high-quality, high-calorie diet. Hares are selective feeders at the best of times: unlike many herbivores, they can't sit around waiting to digest low-quality food – they need high-energy herbs and other leaves in order to sprint. This causes them problems when faced with the smallest alterations in food availability and abundance. So, as well as reductions in the diversity of farmland habitat, the decline in the range of food plants is injurious to hares.

F   The rapid turnaround in the breeding cycle suggests that hares should, in principle, be able to increase their populations quickly to exploit new habitats. They certainly used to: studies show that hares evolved on the open plains and spread rapidly westward from the Black Sea after the last ice age (though they were probably introduced to Britain as a species to be hunted for the pot by the Romans). But today's hares are thwarted by the lack of rich farmland habitat. When the delicate herbs and other plants they rely on are ploughed up or poisoned by herbicides, these wonderful, agile runners disappear too, taking with them some of the wildness from our lives.

Questions 34–36

*Choose the correct letter, **A**, **B**, **C** or **D**.*

Write the correct letter in boxes 34–36 on your answer sheet.

34 According to the writer, what is the ideal habitat for hares?

   A   open grassland which they can run across
   B   densely wooded areas to breed in
   C   areas which include a range of vegetation
   D   land that has been farmed intensively for years

35 When leverets are living alone they are not visited often by their mother because

   A   this helps to protect them from being eaten by other animals.
   B   the 'forms' are so far apart.
   C   they are very energetic from a surprisingly early age.
   D   they know how to find their own food from birth.

36 What does the writer suggest about the adult hares' diet?

   A   They need some plants with a high fat content.
   B   They need time to digest the plants that they eat.
   C   It is difficult for them to adapt to changes in vegetation.
   D   It is vital for them to have a supply of one particular herb.

Questions 37–40

Complete the summary below.

*Choose **ONE WORD ONLY** from the text for each answer.*

Write your answers in boxes 37–40 on your answer sheet.

Brown hares

The brown hare is well known for its ability to run fast, at speeds of up to 70 kph, largely due to the length of its legs as well as the unusual size of its heart. An increased amount of blood also gives it the necessary **37** .... to continue running fast for some time. A running hare resembles the **38** .... more closely than its relative, the rabbit.

The hare has some other characteristics that help it to avoid capture. The first is its excellent all-round **39** .... This means that predators cannot easily creep up behind it. Another feature is its ability to position its massive **40** .... separately, to sense the slightest indication of danger.

WRITING

WRITING TASK 1

You should spend about 20 minutes on this task.

> **You work for an international company. You have seen an advertisement for a training course which will be useful for your job.**
>
> **Write a letter to your manager. In your letter**
> - **describe the training course you want to do**
> - **explain what the company could do to help you**
> - **say how the course will be useful for your job**

Write at least 150 words.

You do **NOT** need to write any addresses.

Begin your letter as follows:

Dear Sir or Madam,

WRITING TASK 2

You should spend about 40 minutes on this task.

Write about the following topic:

> **Some people say that it is possible to tell a lot about a person's culture and character from their choice of clothes.**
>
> **Do you agree or disagree?**

Give reasons for your answer and include any relevant examples from your own knowledge or experience.

Write at least 250 words.

SPEAKING

PART 1

The examiner asks the candidate about him/herself, his/her home, work or studies and other familiar topics.

EXAMPLE

Names

- How did your parents choose your name(s)?
- Does your name have any special meaning?
- Is your name common or unusual in your country?
- If you could change your name, would you? [Why/Why not?]

PART 2

Describe a TV documentary you watched that was particularly interesting.

You should say:
    what the documentary was about
    why you decided to watch it
    what you learnt during the documentary
and explain why the TV documentary was particularly interesting.

You will have to talk about the topic for one to two minutes. You have one minute to think about what you are going to say. You can make some notes to help you if you wish.

PART 3

Discussion topics:

Different types of TV programmes

Example questions:
What are the most popular kinds of TV programmes in your country? Why is this?
Do you think there are too many game shows on TV nowadays? Why?
Do you think TV is the main way for people to get the news in your country? What other ways are there?

TV advertising

Example questions:
What types of products are advertised most often on TV?
Do you think that people pay attention to adverts on TV? Why do you think that is?
How important are regulations on TV advertising?

Audioscripts

SECTION 1

OFFICIAL: Hello?

WOMAN: Oh, hello. I wanted to enquire about hiring a room in the Village Hall, for the evening of September the first.

OFFICIAL: Let me just see … Yes, we have both rooms available that evening. There's our Main Hall – that's got seating for <u>200</u> people. Or there's the Charlton Room … *Example*

WOMAN: Sorry?

OFFICIAL: The <u>Charlton</u> Room – C-H-A-R L-T-O-N. That's got seating for up to one hundred. *Q1*

WOMAN: Well, we're organising a dinner to raise money for a charity, and we're hoping for at least 150 people, so I think we'll go for the Main Hall. How much would that cost?

OFFICIAL: Let's see. You wanted it for the evening of September 1st?

WOMAN: Yes, that's a Saturday.

OFFICIAL: So from six pm to midnight that'd be <u>£115</u> – that's the weekend price, it's £75 on weekdays. *Q2*

WOMAN: That's all right.

OFFICIAL: And I have to tell you there's also a deposit of £250, which is returnable of course as long as there's no damage. But we do insist that this is <u>paid in cash</u>, we don't take cards for that. You can pay the actual rent of the room however you like though – cash, credit card, cheque … *Q3*

WOMAN: Oh, well I suppose that's OK. So does the charge include use of tables and chairs and so on?

OFFICIAL: Oh, yes.

WOMAN: <u>And what about parking?</u>

OFFICIAL: <u>Yeah, that's all included.</u> The only thing that isn't included is … you said you were organising a dinner? *Q4*

WOMAN: Yeah.

OFFICIAL: Well, you'll have to pay extra for the kitchen if you want to use that. It's £25. It's got very good facilities – good quality cookers and fridges and so on.

WOMAN: OK, well I suppose that's all right. We can cover the cost in our entry charges.

OFFICIAL: Right. So I'll make a note of that. Now there are just one or two things you need to think about before the event. For example, <u>you'll have to see about getting a licence if you're planning to have any music during the meal</u>. *Q5*

WOMAN: Oh, really?

OFFICIAL: It's quite straightforward, I'll give you the details later on. And about a week or ten days before your event you'll need to contact the caretaker, that's Mr Evans, <u>to make the arrangements for entry</u> – he'll sort that out with you. *Q6*

WOMAN: And do I give him the payment as well?

OFFICIAL: No, you do that directly with me.

WOMAN: Right. Now is there anything I need to know about what happens during the event?

OFFICIAL: Well, as you'll be aware, of course the building is no smoking throughout.

WOMAN: Of course.

OFFICIAL:	Now, are you having a band?	
WOMAN:	Yes.	
OFFICIAL:	Well, they'll have a lot of equipment, so rather than using the front door they should <u>park their van round the back and use the stage door there</u>. You can open that from inside but don't forget to lock it at the end.	Q7
WOMAN:	OK.	
OFFICIAL:	And talking of bands, I'm sure I don't need to tell you this, but you must make sure that no one fiddles about with the black box by the fire door – that's a system that cuts in when the volume reaches a certain level. It's a legal requirement.	
WOMAN:	Sure. Anyway, we want people to be able to talk to one another so we don't want anything too loud. Oh, that reminds me, we'll be having speeches – are there any microphones available?	
OFFICIAL:	Yeah. Just let the caretaker know, he'll get those for you. Right, now when the event is over we do ask that the premises are left in good condition. So there's <u>a locked cupboard and you'll be informed of the code you need to open that</u>. It's got all the cleaning equipment, brushes and detergent and so on.	Q8
WOMAN:	Right. So what do we need to do after everyone's gone? <u>Sweep the floors I suppose?</u>	
OFFICIAL:	<u>Well, actually they have to be washed, not just swept</u>. Then you'll be provided with black plastic bags, so all the rubbish must be collected up and left outside the door.	Q9
WOMAN:	Of course. We'll make sure everything's left tidy. Oh, and I forgot to ask, <u>I presume we can have decorations in the room?</u>	
OFFICIAL:	<u>Yes, but you must take them down afterwards.</u>	Q10
WOMAN:	Sure.	
OFFICIAL:	And the chairs and tables should be stacked up neatly at the back of the room	
WOMAN:	I'll make sure I've got a few people to help me.	

SECTION 2

Welcome to the Fiddy Working Heritage Farm. This open-air museum gives you the experience of agriculture and rural life in the English countryside at the end of the nineteenth century. So you'll see a typical farm of that period, and like me, all the staff are dressed in clothes of that time.

I must give you some advice and safety tips before we go any further. As it's a *working farm*, please <u>don't frighten or injure the animals</u>. We have a lot here, and many of them are breeds that are now quite rare.   Q11

<u>And do stay at a safe distance from the tools: some of them have sharp points which can be pretty dangerous, so please don't touch them</u>. We don't want any accidents, do we?   Q12

The ground is very uneven, and you might slip if you're wearing sandals so <u>I'm glad to see you're all wearing shoes – we always advise people to do that</u>.   Q13

Now, children of all ages are very welcome here, and usually even very young children love the ducks and lambs, so do bring them along next time you come.

<u>I don't think any of you have brought dogs with you, but in case you have, I'm afraid they'll have to stay in the car park, unless they're guide dogs</u>. I'm sure you'll understand that they could cause a lot of problems on a farm.   Q14

Now let me give you some idea of the layout of the farm. The building where you bought your tickets is the New Barn, immediately to your right, and we're now at the beginning of the main path to the farmland – and of course the car park is on your left. <u>The scarecrow you can see in the car park in the corner, beside the main path</u>, is a traditional figure for keeping the birds away from crops, but our scarecrow is a permanent sculpture. It's taller than a human being, so you can see it from quite a distance.

Q15

<u>If you look ahead of you, you'll see a maze. It's opposite the New Barn, beside the side path that branches off to the right just over there.</u> The maze is made out of hedges which are too tall for young children to see over them, but it's quite small, so you can't get lost in it!

Q16

Now, can you see the bridge crossing the fish pool further up the main path? <u>If you want to go to the café, go towards the bridge and turn right just before it. Walk along the side path and the café's on the first bend you come to.</u> The building was originally the schoolhouse, and it's well over a hundred years old.

Q17

As you may know, we run skills workshops here, where you can learn traditional crafts like woodwork and basket-making. You can see examples of the work, and talk to someone about the courses, in the Black Barn. <u>If you take the side path to the right, here, just by the New Barn, you'll come to the Black Barn just where the path first bends.</u>

Q18

Now I mustn't forget to tell you about picnicking, as I can see some of you have brought your lunch with you. You can picnic in the field, though do clear up behind you, of course. <u>Or if you'd prefer a covered picnic area, there's one near the farmyard: just after you cross the bridge, there's a covered picnic spot on the right</u>.

Q19

And the last thing to mention is <u>Fiddy House itself. From here you can cross the bridge then walk along the footpath through the field to the left of the farmyard. That goes to the house,</u> and it'll give you a lovely view of it. It's certainly worth a few photographs, but as it's a private home, I'm afraid you can't go inside.

Q20

Right. Well, if you're all ready, we'll set off on our tour of the farm.

SECTION 3

LISA: OK, Greg, so I finally managed to read the article you mentioned – the one about the study on gender in physics.

GREG: About the study of college students done by Akira Miyake and his team? Yeah. I was interested that the researchers were actually a mix of psychologists and physicists. That's an unusual combination.

LISA: Yeah. I got a little confused at first about which students the study was based on. They weren't actually majoring in physics – <u>they were majoring in what's known as the STEM disciplines. That's science, technology, engineering and …</u>

Q21

GREG: … <u>and math.</u> Yes, but they were all doing physics courses as part of their studies.

LISA: That's correct. So as I understood it, Miyake and co started from the fact that women are underrepresented in introductory physics courses at college, and also that on average, the women who do enrol on these courses perform more poorly than the men. No one really knows why this is the case.

GREG: Yeah. <u>But what the researchers wanted to find out was basically what they could do about the relatively low level of the women's results.</u> But in order to find a solution they needed to find out more about the nature of the problem.

Q22

LISA: Right – now let's see if I can remember … it was that in the physics class, the female students thought the male students all assumed that women weren't any good at physics … was that it? And they thought that the men expected them to get poor results in their tests.

GREG: That's what the women thought, and that made them nervous, so they did get poor results. <u>But actually they were wrong … No one was making any assumptions about the female students at all</u>. *Q23*

LISA: Anyway, what Miyake's team did was quite simple – getting the students to do some writing before they went into the physics class. What did they call it?

GREG: Values-affirmation – <u>they had to write an essay focusing on things that were significant to them, not particularly to do with the subject they were studying, but more general things like music, or people who mattered to them</u>. *Q24*

LISA: Right. So the idea of doing the writing is that this gets the students thinking in a positive way.

GREG: <u>And putting these thoughts into words can relax them and help them overcome the psychological factors that lead to poor performance</u>. Yeah. <u>But what the researchers in the study hadn't expected was that this one activity raised the women's physics grades from the C to the B range</u>. *Q25* *Q26*

LISA: A huge change. Pity it wasn't to an A, but still! No, but it does suggest that the women were seriously underperforming beforehand, in comparison with the men.

GREG: Yes. Mind you, Miyake's article left out a lot of details. Like, did the students do the writing just once, or several times? <u>And had they been told why they were doing the writing? That might have affected the results</u>. *Q27*

LISA: You mean, if they know the researchers thought it might help them to improve, then they'd just try to fulfil that expectation?

GREG: Exactly.

GREG: So anyway, I thought for our project we could do a similar study, but investigate whether it really was the writing activity that had that result.

LISA: OK. So we could ask them to do a writing task about something completely different … something more factual? Like a general knowledge topic.

GREG: Maybe … or we could have half the students doing a writing task and half doing something else, like an oral task.

LISA: Or even, <u>half do the same writing task as in the original research and half do a factual writing task</u>. Then we'd see if it really is the topic that made the difference, or something else. *Q28*

GREG: That's it. Good. So at our meeting with the supervisor on Monday we can tell him we've decided on our project. We should have our aims ready by then. I suppose we need to read the original study – the article's just a summary.

LISA: And there was another article I read, by Smolinsky. It was about her research on how women and men perform in mixed teams in class, compared with single-sex teams and on their own.

GREG: Let me guess … the women were better at teamwork.

LISA: That's what I expected, but actually <u>the men and the women got the same results whether they were working in teams or on their own</u>. But I guess it's not that relevant to us. *Q29*

GREG: What worries me anyway is how we're going to get everything done in the time.

LISA: We'll be OK now we know what we're doing. Though I'm not clear how we assess whether the students in our experiment actually make any progress or not …

GREG: No. We may need some advice on that. The main thing's to make sure we have the right size sample, not too big or too small.

LISA: That shouldn't be difficult. Right, what do we need to do next? We could have a look at the timetable for the science classes … or perhaps <u>we should just make an appointment to see one of the science professors. That'd be better</u>. *Q30*

GREG: Great. And we could even get to observe one of the classes.

LISA: What for?

GREG: Well … OK maybe let's just go with your idea. Right, well …

SECTION 4

I've been looking at ocean biodiversity, that's the diversity of species that live in the world's oceans. About 20 years ago biologists developed the idea of what they called 'biodiversity hotspots'. These are the areas which have the greatest mixture of species, so one example is Madagascar. <u>These hotspots are significant because they allow us to locate key areas for focusing efforts at conservation</u>. Biologists can identify hotspots on land, fairly easily, but until recently, very little was known about species distribution and diversity in the oceans, and no one even knew if hotspots existed there.

Q31

Then a Canadian biologist called Boris Worm did some research in 2005 on data on ocean species that he got from the fishing industry. Worm located five hotspots for large ocean predators like sharks, and looked at what they had in common. <u>The main thing he'd expected to find was that they had very high concentrations of food, but to his surprise that was only true for four of the hotspots – the remaining hotspot was quite badly off in that regard</u>. But what he did find was that in all cases, the <u>water at the surface of the ocean had relatively high temperatures, even when it was cool at greater depths</u>, so this seemed to be a factor in supporting a diverse range of these large predators. However, this wasn't enough on its own, <u>because he also found that the water needed to have enough oxygen in it</u> – so these two factors seemed necessary to support the high metabolic rate of these large fish.

Q32

Q33

Q34

A couple of years later, in 2007, a researcher called Lisa Ballance, who was working in California, also started looking for ocean hotspots, but not for fish – <u>what she was interested in was marine mammals, things like seals</u>. And she found three places in the oceans which were hotspots, and what these had in common was that these hotspots were all located at boundaries between ocean currents, and this seems to be the sort of place that has lots of the plankton that some of these species feed on.

Q35

So now people who want to protect the species that are endangered need to get as much information as possible. For example, there's an international project called the Census of Marine Life. They've been surveying oceans all over the world, including the Arctic. <u>One thing they found there which stunned other researchers was that there were large numbers of species which live below the ice</u> – sometimes under a layer up to 20 metres thick. Some of these species had never been seen before. They've even found species of octopus living in these conditions. And other scientists working on the same project, but researching very different habitats on the ocean floor, have found large numbers of species congregating around volcanoes, attracted to them by the warmth and nutrients there.

Q36

However, biologists still don't know how serious the threat to their survival is for each individual species. So a body called the Global Marine Species Assessment is now creating a list of endangered species on land, so they consider things like the size of the population – how many members of one species there are in a particular place – and then they look at their distribution in geographical terms, although this is quite difficult when you're looking at fish, because they're so mobile, and then <u>thirdly they calculate the rate at which the decline of the species is happening</u>.

Q37

So far only 1,500 species have been assessed, but they want to increase this figure to 20,000. <u>For each one they assess, they use the data they collect on that species to produce a map showing its distribution</u>. Ultimately they will be able to use these to figure out not only where most species are located but also where they are most threatened.

Q38

So finally, what can be done to retain the diversity of species in the world's oceans? Firstly, we need to set up more reserves in our oceans, places where marine species are protected. We have some, but not enough. In addition, to preserve species such as leatherback turtles,

which live out in the high seas but have their nesting sites on the American coast, <u>we need</u> *Q39*
<u>to create corridors for migration</u>, so they can get from one area to another safely. As well as this, action needs to be taken to lower the levels of fishing quotas to prevent overfishing of endangered species. And finally, there's the problem of 'by-catch'. This refers to the catching of unwanted fish by fishing boats – they're returned to the sea, but they're often dead or dying. If these commercial fishing boats used equipment which was more selective, <u>so that</u> *Q40*
<u>only the fish wanted for consumption were caught</u>, this problem could be overcome.

OK. So does anyone have any …

TEST 2

SECTION 1

CAROLINE: Good Morning. Youth Council. Caroline speaking.

ROGER: Oh, hello, I'm interested in standing for election to the Youth Council, and I was told to give you a call.

CAROLINE: That's good. Could I have your name, please?

ROGER: Yes, it's Roger <u>Brown</u>. *Example*

CAROLINE: Thank you. I'm Caroline, the Youth Council administrator. So do you know much about what the Council does, Roger?

ROGER: I've talked to Stephanie – I think she's the chair of the Council.

CAROLINE: That's right.

ROGER: And she told me a lot about it. How it's a way for young people to discuss local issues, for example, and make suggestions to the town council. That's what made me interested.

CAROLINE: Fine. Well let me take down some of your details. First of all, how old are you? You know the Council is for young people aged from 13 to 18?

ROGER: I've just turned 18.

CAROLINE: And where do you live, Roger?

ROGER: Well, that's a bit complicated. At the moment I'm looking for a flat to rent here, so <u>I'm in a hostel from Monday to Friday</u>. I go back to my parents' place at the *Q1* weekend.

CAROLINE: OK, so where's the best place to send you some information about the Council?

ROGER: Oh, to my parents' address, please. That's 17, <u>Buckleigh</u> Street – B-U-C-K-L-E-I- *Q2* G-H Street, Stamford, Lincolnshire, though you don't really need the county.

CAROLINE: Oh, I know Stamford – it's a lovely town. And what's the postcode?

ROGER: <u>PE9 7QT</u> *Q3*

CAROLINE: Right, thank you. So are you working here, or are you a student?

ROGER: I started studying at the university a couple of weeks ago, and I've got a part-time job for a few hours a week.

CAROLINE: What do you do?

ROGER: Well, I've done several different things. I've just finished a short-term contract as a courier, and now <u>I'm working as a waiter</u> in one of the big hotels. *Q4*

CAROLINE: Uhuh. That can't leave you much time for studying!

ROGER: Oh, it's not too bad. I manage to fit it all in.

CAROLINE: What are you studying?

ROGER: My ambition is to go into parliament eventually, so <u>my major subject is politics</u>. *Q5* That's partly why I think the Youth Council is important and want to be a part of it.

CAROLINE: And I suppose you're also taking a minor subject, aren't you? I know a lot of people study economics too.

ROGER: I chose history. To be honest, I'm not finding it as interesting as I expected!

CAROLINE: OK, so with your studying and your part-time job, do you have time for any other interests or hobbies?

ROGER: Well, <u>I spend quite a lot of time cycling</u> – both around town to get to university and to work, and also long-distance, from here to London, for instance.   *Q6*

CAROLINE: That's pretty impressive! Anything else?

ROGER: For relaxation <u>I'm also keen on the cinema</u> – I used to go at least once a week, but I can't manage to go so often now.   *Q7*

CAROLINE: Right. Are you sure you'll have enough time for the Youth Council?

ROGER: Yes, I've worked out that I can afford to reduce my hours at work, and that will make the time.

CAROLINE: So is there any particular aspect of the Youth Council's work that appeals to you, Roger?

ROGER: Well, my sister is blind, so <u>I'm particularly interested in working with disabled young people</u>, to try and improve the quality of their lives.   *Q8*

CAROLINE: That's great. Well, the best way to get involved is to be nominated by some people who you know.

ROGER: Right. Can you tell me how to set about organising that?

CAROLINE: You should talk to Jeffrey, our Elections Officer. I can arrange a meeting in the council office with him, if you like.

ROGER: Yes, please.

CAROLINE: He'll be here next Monday, if that suits you.

ROGER: That's the 14th, isn't it?

CAROLINE: Yes.

ROGER: I can manage late afternoon.

CAROLINE: Would you like to suggest a time? He generally leaves around 5.30.

ROGER: Well, <u>would 4.30 be OK</u>? My last class finishes at 4, so I'd have plenty of time to get to your office.   *Q9*

CAROLINE: Right, that's fine. Oh, and could I have a phone number we can contact you on?

ROGER: Yes, <u>my mobile number's 07788 136711</u>.   *Q10*

CAROLINE: Thank you. Well, we'll look forward to seeing you next week.

ROGER: Thanks very much. Goodbye.

CAROLINE: Bye.

SECTION 2

Hi. Great to see you! I'm Jody, and I'll be looking after both of you for the first month you're working here at the Amersham Theatre. I'll tell you something about the theatre now, then take you to meet two of the other staff.

It's an old building, and it's been modernised several times. In fact, as you can see, we're carrying out a major refurbishment at the moment. The interior has just been repainted, and we're about to start on the exterior of the building – that'll be a big job. The work's running over budget, so we've had to postpone installing an elevator. I hope you're happy running up and down stairs! When the theatre was built, people were generally slimmer and shorter than now, and the seats were very close together. <u>We've replaced them with larger seats,</u>   *Q11 & 12* <u>with more legroom. This means fewer seats in total, but we've taken the opportunity to install</u> <u>seats that can easily be moved</u>, to create different acting spaces. <u>We've also turned a few</u>   *Q11 & 12* storerooms over to other purposes, like using them for meetings.

We try hard to involve members of the public in the theatre. One way is by organising backstage tours, so people can be shown round the building and learn how a theatre operates. These are proving very popular. What we're finding is that people want to have lunch or a cup of coffee while they're here, so we're looking into the possibility of opening a café in due course. We have a bookshop, which specialises in books about drama, and that attracts plenty of customers. Then there are two large rooms that will be decorated next month, and they'll be available for hire, for conferences and private functions, such as parties. We're also considering hiring out costumes to amateur drama clubs.

Q13 & 14

Q13 & 14

Now I want to tell you about our workshops. We recently started a programme of workshops that anyone can join. Eventually we intend to run courses in acting, but we're waiting until we've got the right people in place as trainers. That's proving more difficult than we'd expected! There's a big demand to learn about the technical side of putting on a production, and our lighting workshop has already started, with great success. We're going to start one on sound next month. A number of people have enquired about workshops on make-up, and that's something we're considering for the future. A surprise success is the workshop on making puppets – we happen to have someone working here who does it as a hobby, and she offered to run a workshop. It was so popular we're now running them every month!

Q15 & 16

Q15 & 16

Now, a word about the layout of the building. The auditorium, stage and dressing rooms for the actors are all below ground level. Here on the ground floor we have most of the rooms that the public doesn't see. The majority are internal, so they have windows in the roof to light them.

Standing here in the foyer, you're probably wondering why the box office isn't here, where the public would expect to find it. Well, you might have noticed it on your way in – although it's part of this building, it's next door, with a separate entrance from the road.

Q17

For the theatre manager's office, you go across the foyer and through the double doors, turn right, and it's the room at the end of the corridor, with the door on the left.

Q18

The lighting box is where the computerised stage lighting is operated, and it's at the back of the building. When you're through the double doors, turn left, turn right at the water cooler, and right again at the end. It's the second room along that corridor. The lighting box has a window into the auditorium, which of course is below us.

Q19

The artistic director's office is through the double doors, turn right, and it's the first room you come to on the right-hand side. And finally, for the moment, the room where I'll take you next – the relaxation room. So if you'd like to come with me …

Q20

SECTION 3

HELEN: I've brought my notes on our Biology Field Trip to Rocky Bay, Colin, so we can work on our report on the research we did together.

COLIN: OK. I've got mine too. Let's look at the aims of the trip first.

HELEN: Right. What did you have?

COLIN: I just put something about getting experience of the different sorts of procedures used on a field trip. But we need something about what causes different organisms to choose particular habitats.

Q21

HELEN: I agree. And something about finding out how to protect organisms in danger of dying out?

COLIN:	In our aims? But we weren't really looking at that.
HELEN:	I suppose not. OK, now there's the list of equipment we all had to bring on the field trip. What did they tell us to bring a ruler for?
COLIN:	It was something about measuring the slope of the shore, but of course we didn't need it because we were measuring wind direction, and we'd brought the compass for that …
HELEN:	<u>But not the piece of string to hold up in the air! Didn't Mr Blake make a fuss about us leaving that behind</u>.
COLIN:	Yeah. He does go on. Anyway it was easy to get one from another of the students.
HELEN:	Now, the next section's the procedure. I sent you the draft of that.
COLIN:	Yeah. It was clear, but <u>I don't think we need all these details of what time we left and what time we got back and how we divided up the different research tasks</u>.
HELEN:	OK. I'll look at that again.
COLIN:	Then we have to describe our method of investigation in detail. <u>So let's begin with how we measured wave speed. I was surprised how straightforward that was</u>.
HELEN:	<u>I'd expected us to have some sort of high-tech device, not just stand there and count the number of waves per minute</u>. Not very precise, but I suppose it was good enough. But the way we measured the amount of salt was interesting.
COLIN:	In the water from the rock pools?
HELEN:	Yeah, oh, I wanted to check the chemicals we used in the lab when we analysed those samples – was it potassium chromate and silver nitrate?
COLIN:	That's right.
HELEN:	OK. And we need the map of the seashore. You just left that to me. And I had to do it while the tide was low, well that was OK, but <u>the place I started it from was down on the beach, then I realised I should have gone up higher to get better visibility</u>, so I had to start all over again. But at least I'd got the squared paper or I'd have had problems drawing it all to scale.
COLIN:	Yes. It looks good. We could get a map of the region off the internet and see if we need to make any changes.
HELEN:	I had a look but I couldn't find anything. But you took some pictures, didn't you?
COLIN:	Yeah. I'll email you them if you want.
HELEN:	OK. <u>I'll make my amendments using those, then I can scan it into our report.</u> Great.

Q22

Q23

Q24

Q25

Q26

HELEN:	Now when we get to our findings I thought we could divide them up into the different zones we identified on the shore and the problems organisms face in each zone. So for the highest area …
COLIN:	… the splash zone?
HELEN:	Yeah, we found mostly those tiny shellfish that have strong hard shells that act as protection.
COLIN:	But not from other organisms that might eat them, predators?
HELEN:	No, that's not the main danger for them. <u>But the shells prevent them from drying out because they're in the open air for most of the time</u>.
COLIN:	Right. And since they're exposed, they need to be able to find some sort of shelter, or cover themselves up, <u>so they don't get too hot</u>. Then in the middle and lower zones, nearer the sea, we need to discuss the effects of wave action …
HELEN:	Yes, and how organisms develop structures to prevent themselves from being swept away, or even destroyed by being smashed against the rocks.
COLIN:	I haven't done anything on the geological changes. I don't know what to put for that.
HELEN:	No, we weren't concentrating on that. Maybe we need to find some websites.
COLIN:	Good idea. I've got the lecture notes from Mr Blake's geology course, but they're too general. But we could ask him which books on our Reading List might be most helpful.

Q27 & 28

Q27 & 28

HELEN: Right. OK, now I did a draft of the section of sources of possible error in our research, but I don't know if you agree. For example, the size of the sample, and whether it's big enough to make any general conclusions from. But I thought actually we did have quite a big sample.

COLIN: We did. And our general method of observation seemed quite reliable. But we might not be all that accurate as far as the actual numbers go.

HELEN: Yeah, <u>we might have missed some organisms – if they were hiding under a rock, for example</u>. I wasn't sure about the way we described their habitats. I decided it was probably OK.   *Q29 & 30*

COLIN: Yeah, and the descriptions we gave of the smaller organisms, they weren't very detailed, but they were adequate in this context. <u>I'm not sure we identified all the species correctly though</u>.   *Q29 & 30*

HELEN: OK, we'd better mention that. Now, how …

SECTION 4

We've been discussing the factors the architect has to consider when designing domestic buildings. I'm going to move on now to consider the design of *public* buildings, and I'll illustrate this by referring to the new Taylor Concert Hall that's recently been completed here in the city.

So, as with a domestic building, when designing a public building, an architect needs to consider the function of the building – for example, is it to be used primarily for entertainment, or for education, or for administration? The second thing the architect needs to think about is the context of the building, <u>this includes its physical location, obviously, but it also includes the social meaning of the building, how it relates to the people it's built for</u>. And finally, for important public buildings, the architect may also be looking for a central symbolic idea on which to base the design, a sort of metaphor for the building and the way in which it is used.   *Q31*

Let's look at the new Taylor Concert Hall in relation to these ideas. <u>The location chosen was a site in a run-down district that has been ignored in previous redevelopment plans. It was occupied by a factory that had been empty for some years</u>. The whole area was some distance from the high-rise office blocks of the central business district and shopping centre, but it was only one kilometre from the ring road. <u>The site itself was bordered to the north by a canal</u> which had once been used by boats bringing in raw materials when the area was used for manufacturing.   *Q32*   *Q33*

The architect chosen for the project was Tom Harrison. He found the main design challenge was the location of the site in an area that had no neighbouring buildings of any importance. To reflect the fact that the significance of the building in this quite run-down location was as yet unknown, he decided to create a building centred around the idea of a mystery – something whose meaning still has to be discovered.

So how was this reflected in the design of the building? Well, Harrison decided to create pedestrian access to the building and to make use of the presence of water on the site. <u>As people approach the entrance, they therefore have to cross over a bridge</u>. He wanted to give people a feeling of suspense as they see the building first from a distance, and then close-up, and <u>the initial impression he wanted to create from the shape of the building as a whole was that of a box</u>. The first side that people see, the southern wall, is just a high, flat wall uninterrupted by any windows. This might sound off-putting, but it supports Harrison's concept of the building – that the person approaching is intrigued and wonders what will be inside. <u>And this flat wall also has another purpose. At night-time, projectors are switched on and it functions as a huge screen, onto which images are projected</u>.   *Q34*   *Q35*   *Q36*

The auditorium itself seats 1500 people. <u>The floor's supported by ten massive pads.</u> Q37
<u>These are constructed from rubber</u>, and so are able to absorb any vibrations from outside
and prevent them from affecting the auditorium. The walls are made of several layers of
honey-coloured wood, all sourced from local beech trees. In order to improve the acoustic
properties of the auditorium and to amplify the sound, <u>they are not straight, they are curved</u>. Q38
The acoustics are also adjustable according to the size of orchestra and the type of music
being played. In order to achieve this, there are nine movable panels in the ceiling above the
orchestra which are all individually motorized, and <u>the walls also have curtains which can be</u> Q39
<u>opened or closed to change the acoustics</u>.

The reaction of the public to the new building has generally been positive. <u>However, the</u> Q40
<u>evaluation of some critics has been less enthusiastic. In spite of Harrison's efforts to use local</u>
<u>materials, they criticise the style of the design as being international rather than local</u>, and
say it doesn't reflect features of the landscape or society for which it is built.

TEST 3

SECTION 1

MARTIN: Good morning. This is Burnham tourist office, Martin speaking.

SUE: Oh, hello. I saw a poster about free things to do in the area, and it said people should
phone you for information. I'm coming to Burnham with my husband and two children
for a few days on June the 27th, or possibly the 28th, and <u>I'd like some ideas for</u> *Example*
<u>things to do on the 29th.</u>

MARTIN: Yes, of course. OK. Then let's start with a couple of events especially for children.
The art gallery is holding an event called 'Family Welcome' that day, when there are
activities and trails to use throughout the gallery.

SUE: That sounds interesting. What time does it start?

MARTIN: The gallery opens at 10, and <u>the 'Family Welcome' event runs from 10.30 until 2</u> Q1
<u>o'clock</u>. The gallery stays open until 5. And several times during the day, <u>they're</u> Q2
<u>going to show a short film that the gallery has produced. It demonstrates how</u>
<u>ceramics are made</u>, and there'll be equipment and materials for children to have a go
themselves. Last time they ran the event, there was a film about painting, which went
down very well with the children, and they're now working on one about sculpture.

SUE: I like the sound of that. And what other events happen in Burnham?

MARTIN: Well, do you all enjoy listening to music?

SUE: Oh, yes.

MARTIN: Well there are several free concerts taking place at different times – one or two in the
morning, <u>the majority at lunchtime</u>, and a couple in the evening. And they range from Q3
pop music to Latin American.

SUE: The Latin American could be fun. What time is that?

MARTIN: It's being repeated several times, in different places. They're performing in the central
library at 1 o'clock, <u>then at 4 it's in the City Museum</u>, and in the evening, at 7.30, Q4
there's a longer concert, in the theatre.

SUE: Right. I'll suggest that to the rest of the family.

MARTIN: Something else you might be interested in is the boat race along the river.

SUE: Oh, yes, do tell me about that.

MARTIN: <u>The race starts at Offord Marina</u>, to the north of Burnham, and goes as far as Q5
Summer Pool. The best place to watch it from is Charlesworth Bridge, though that
does get rather crowded.

SUE:	And who's taking part?	
MARTIN:	Well, local boat clubs, but the standard is very high. <u>One of them came first in the West of England regional championship in May this year</u> – it was the first time a team from Burnham has won. It means that next year they'll be representing the region in the national championship.	*Q6*

SUE:	Now I've heard something about Paxton Nature Reserve. <u>It's a good place for spotting unusual birds, isn't it?</u>	*Q7*
MARTIN:	<u>That's right – throughout the year.</u> There is a lake there, as well as a river, and they provide a very attractive habitat. So it's a good idea to bring binoculars if you have them. <u>And just at the moment you can see various flowers that are pretty unusual</u> – the soil at Paxton isn't very common. They're looking good right now.	*Q8*
SUE:	Right. My husband will be particularly interested in that.	
MARTIN:	<u>And there's going to be a talk and slide show about mushrooms – and you'll be able to go out and pick some afterwards and study the different varieties.</u>	*Q9*
SUE:	Uhuh. And is it possible for children to swim in the river?	
MARTIN:	Yes. <u>Part of it has been fenced off to make it safe for children to swim in.</u> It's very shallow, and there's a lifeguard on duty whenever it's open. The lake is too deep, so swimming isn't allowed there.	*Q10*
SUE:	OK, we must remember to bring their swimming things, in case we go to Paxton. How long does it take to get there by car from Burnham?	
MARTIN:	About 20 minutes, but parking is very limited, so it's usually much easier to go by bus – and it takes about the same time.	
SUE:	Right. Well, I'll discuss the options with the rest of the family. Thanks very much for all your help.	
MARTIN:	You're welcome.	
SUE:	Goodbye.	
MARTIN:	Bye.	

SECTION 2

MAN:	First of all, let me thank you all for coming to this public meeting, to discuss the future of our town. Our first speaker is Shona Ferguson, from Barford town council. Shona.
SHONA:	Thank you. First I'll briefly give you some background information, then I'll be asking you for your comments on developments in the town.

Well, as you don't need me to tell you, Barford has changed a great deal in the last 50 years. These are some of the main changes.

Fifty years ago, buses linked virtually every part of the town and the neighbouring towns and villages. Most people used them frequently, <u>but not now, because the bus companies concentrate on just the routes that attract most passengers. So parts of the town are no longer served by buses.</u> Even replacing old uncomfortable buses with smart new ones has had little impact on passenger numbers. It's sometimes said that bus fares are too high, but in relation to average incomes, fares are not much higher than they were 50 years ago.   *Q11*

Changes in the road network are affecting the town. The centre was recently closed to traffic on a trial basis, making it much safer for pedestrians. The impact of this is being measured. <u>The new cycle paths, separating bikes from cars in most main roads, are being used far more than was expected, reducing traffic and improving air quality.</u> And although the council's attempts to have a bypass constructed have failed, we haven't given up hope of persuading the government to change its mind.   *Q12*

Shopping in the town centre has changed over the years. Many of us can remember when the town was crowded with people going shopping. Numbers have been falling for several years, despite efforts to attract shoppers, for instance by opening new car parks. Some people combine shopping with visits to the town's restaurants and cafés. Most shops are small independent stores, which is good, but <u>many people prefer to use supermarkets and department stores in nearby large towns, as there are so few well-known chain stores here</u>. Q13

Turning now to medical facilities, the town is served by family doctors in several medical practices – fewer than 50 years ago, but each catering for far more patients. <u>Our hospital closed 15 years ago</u>, which means journeys to other towns are unavoidable. On the other hand, there are more dentists than there used to be. Q14

Employment patterns have changed, along with almost everything else. <u>The number of schools and colleges has increased, making that the main employment sector</u>. Services, such as website design and accountancy, have grown in importance, and surprisingly, perhaps, manufacturing hasn't seen the decline that has affected it in other parts of the country. Q15

Now I'll very quickly outline current plans for some of the town's facilities, before asking for your comments.

As you'll know if you regularly use the car park at the railway station, it's usually full. The railway company applied for permission to replace it with a multi-storey car park, but that was refused. <u>Instead, the company has bought some adjoining land, and this will be used to increase the number of parking spaces</u>. Q16

<u>The Grand, the old cinema in the high street, will close at the end of the year, and reopen on a different site</u>. You've probably seen the building under construction. The plan is to have three screens with fewer seats, rather than just the one large auditorium in the old cinema. Q17

I expect many of you shop in the indoor market. It's become more and more shabby-looking, and because of fears about safety, it was threatened with demolition. <u>The good news is that it will close for six weeks to be made safe and redecorated, and the improved building will open in July</u>. Q18

Lots of people use the library, including school and college students who go there to study. <u>The council has managed to secure funding to keep the library open later into the evening, twice a week</u>. We would like to enlarge the building in the not-too-distant future, but this is by no means definite. Q19

There's no limit on access to the nature reserve on the edge of town, and this will continue to be the case. What *will* change, though, is that the council will no longer be in charge of the area. <u>Instead it will become the responsibility of a national body that administers most nature reserves in the country</u>. Q20

OK, now let me ask you …

SECTION 3

JEREMY: Hello, Helen. Sorry I'm late.

HELEN: Hi, Jeremy, no problem. Well we'd better work out where we are on our project, I suppose.

JEREMY: Yeah. I've looked at the drawings you've done for my story, 'The Forest', and I think they're brilliant – they really create the atmosphere I had in mind when I was writing it.

HELEN: I'm glad you like them.

JEREMY: There are just a few suggestions I'd like to make.

HELEN: Go ahead.

JEREMY: Now, I'm not sure about <u>the drawing of the cave – it's got trees all around it</u>, which is great, but the drawing's a bit too static, isn't it? I think it needs some action. Q21

HELEN: Yes, there's nothing happening. Perhaps I should add the boy – Malcolm, isn't it? He would be walking up to it.

JEREMY: Yes, let's have Malcolm in the drawing. And what about putting in a tiger – the one that he makes friends with a bit later? Maybe it could be sitting under a tree washing itself.   Q22

HELEN: And the tiger stops in the middle of what it's doing when it sees Malcolm walking past.

JEREMY: That's a good idea.

HELEN: OK, I'll have a go at that.

JEREMY: Then there's the drawing of the crowd of men and women dancing. They're just outside the forest, and there's a lot going on.   Q23

HELEN: That's right, you wanted them to be watching a carnival procession, but I thought it would be too crowded. Do you think it works like this?

JEREMY: Yes, I like what you've done. The only thing is, could you add Malcolm to it, without changing what's already there.

HELEN: What about having him sitting on the tree trunk on the right of the picture?

JEREMY: Yes, that would be fine.

HELEN: And do you want him watching the other people?

JEREMY: No, he's been left out of all the fun, so I'd like him to be crying – that'll contrast nicely with the next picture, where he's laughing at the clowns in the carnival.   Q24

HELEN: Right, I'll do that.

JEREMY: And then the drawing of the people ice skating in the forest.

HELEN: I wasn't too happy with that one. Because they're supposed to be skating on grass, aren't they?   Q25

JEREMY: That's right, and it's frozen over. At the moment it doesn't look quite right.

HELEN: Mm, I see what you mean. I'll have another go at that.

JEREMY: And I like the wool hats they're wearing. Maybe you could give each of them a scarf, as well.   Q26

HELEN: Yeah, that's easy enough. They can be streaming out behind the people to suggest they're skating really fast.

JEREMY: Mm, great. Well that's all on the drawings.

HELEN: Right. So you've finished writing your story and I just need to finish illustrating it, and my story and your drawings are done.

HELEN: So the next thing is to decide what exactly we need to write about in the report that goes with the stories, and how we're going to divide the work.

JEREMY: Right, Helen.

HELEN: What do you think about including a section on how we planned the project as a whole, Jeremy? That's probably quite important.

JEREMY: Yeah. Well, you've had most of the good ideas so far. How do you feel about drafting something, then we can go through it together and discuss it?   Q27

HELEN: OK, that seems reasonable. And I could include something on how we came up with the ideas for our two stories, couldn't I?

JEREMY: Well I've started writing something about that, so why don't you do the same and we can include the two things.   Q28

HELEN: Right. So what about our interpretation of the stories? Do we need to write about what we think they show, like the value of helping other people, all that sort of thing?

JEREMY: That's going to come up later, isn't it? I think everyone in the class is going to read each other's stories and come up with their own interpretations, which we're going to discuss.   Q29

HELEN: Oh, I missed that. So it isn't going to be part of the report at all?

JEREMY: No. But we need to write about the illustrations, because they're an essential element of children's experience of reading the stories. It's probably easiest for you to write that section, as you know more about drawing than I do.

HELEN: Maybe, but I find it quite hard to write about. <u>I'd be happier if you did it.</u>   *Q30*

JEREMY: OK. So when do you think …

SECTION 4

So what I'm going to talk about to you today is something called Ethnography. This is a type of research aimed at exploring the way human cultures work. It was first developed for use in anthropology, and it's also been used in sociology and communication studies. So what's it got to do with business, you may ask. Well, businesses are finding that <u>ethnography can offer</u>   *Q31* <u>them deeper insight into the possible needs of customers, either present or future, as well as</u> <u>providing valuable information about their attitudes towards existing products</u>. And ethnography can also help companies to design new products or services that customers really want.

Let's look at some examples of how ethnographic research works in business. One team of researchers did a project for a company manufacturing kitchen equipment. They watched how cooks used measuring cups to measure out things like sugar and flour. They saw that the cooks had to check and recheck the contents, because <u>although the measuring cups</u>   *Q32* <u>had numbers inside them, the cooks couldn't see these easily</u>. So a new design of cup was developed to overcome this problem, and it was a top seller.

Another team of ethnographic researchers looked at how cell phones were used in Uganda, in Africa. They found that people who didn't have their own phones could pay to use the phones of local entrepreneurs. Because these customers paid in advance for their calls, <u>they</u>   *Q33* <u>were eager to know how much time they'd spent on the call so far</u>. So the phone company designed phones for use globally with this added feature.

Ethnographic research has also been carried out in computer companies. In one company, IT systems administrators were observed for several weeks. It was found that a large amount of their work involved communicating with colleagues in order to solve problems, but that <u>they</u>   *Q34* <u>didn't have a standard way of exchanging information from spreadsheets and so on. So the</u> <u>team came up with an idea for software that would help them to do this</u>.

In another piece of research, a team observed and talked to nurses working in hospitals. <u>This led to the recognition that the nurses needed to access the computer records of their</u>   *Q35* <u>patients, no matter where they were</u>. This led to the development of a portable computer tablet that allowed the nurses to check records in locations throughout the hospital.

Occasionally, research can be done even in environments where the researchers can't be present. For example, in one project done for an airline, <u>respondents used their smartphones</u>   *Q36* <u>to record information during airline trips, in a study aiming at tracking the emotions of</u> <u>passengers during a flight</u>.

So what makes studies like these different from ordinary research? Let's look at some of the general principles behind ethnographic research in business. First of all, the researcher has to be completely open-minded – he or she hasn't thought up a hypothesis to be tested, as is the case in other types of research. Instead they wait for the participants in the research to inform them. As far as choosing the participants themselves is concerned, that's not really all that different from ordinary research – the criteria according to which the participants are chosen may be something as simple as the age bracket they fall into, <u>or the researchers may select</u>   *Q37* <u>them according to their income</u>, or they might try to find a set of people who all use a particular product, for example. But it's absolutely crucial to recruit the right people as participants. As well as the criteria I've mentioned, <u>they have to be comfortable talking about themselves and being watched as they go about their activities</u>. Actually, most researchers say that people open up pretty easily, maybe because they're often in their own home or workplace.   *Q38*

So what makes this type of research special is that it's not just a matter of sending a questionnaire to the participants, instead <u>the research is usually based on first-hand observation of what they are doing at the time</u>. But that doesn't mean that the researcher never talks to the participants. However, unlike in traditional research, in this case it's the participant rather than the researchers who decides what direction the interview will follow. This means that there's less likelihood of the researcher imposing his or her own ideas on the participant.   *Q39*

But after they've said goodbye to their participants and got back to their office, the researchers' work isn't finished. <u>Most researchers estimate that 70 to 80 per cent of their time is spent not on the collecting of data but on its analysis – looking at photos, listening to recordings and transcribing them, and so on</u>. The researchers may end up with hundreds of pages of notes. And to determine what's significant, they don't focus on the sensational things or the unusual things, instead they try to identify a pattern of some sort in all this data, and to discern the meaning behind it. This can result in some compelling insights that can in turn feed back to the whole design process.   *Q40*

TEST 4

SECTION 1

ROB: Good morning. Stretton Festival box office. How can I help you?

MELANIE: Oh, hello. My family and I are on holiday in the area, and we've seen some posters about the festival this week. Could you tell me about some of the events, please?

ROB: Of course.

MELANIE: First of all, are there still tickets available for the jazz band on Saturday?

ROB: There are, but only £15. The £12 seats have all been sold.   *Example*

MELANIE: OK. And the venue is the school, isn't it?

ROB: Yes, that's right, <u>the secondary school</u>. Make sure you don't go to the primary school   *Q1* by mistake! And there's an additional performer who isn't mentioned on the posters – Carolyn Hart is going to play with the band.

MELANIE: Oh, I think I've heard her on the radio. Doesn't she play the oboe, or flute or something?

ROB: <u>Yes, the flute</u>. She usually plays with symphony orchestras, and apparently this is   *Q2* her first time with a jazz band.

MELANIE: Well, I'd certainly like to hear *her*. Then the next thing I want to ask about is the duck races – I saw a poster beside a river. What are they, exactly?

ROB: Well, you buy a yellow plastic duck – or as many as you like – they're a pound each. And you write your name on each one. There'll be several races, depending on the number of ducks taking part. And John Stevens, a champion swimmer who lives locally, is going to start the races. <u>All the ducks will be launched into the river at the   *Q3* back of the cinema</u>, then they'll float along the river for 500 metres, as far as the railway bridge.

MELANIE: And are there any prizes?

ROB:	Yes, <u>the first duck in each race to arrive at the finishing line wins its owner free tickets for the concert on the last night of the festival</u>.	Q4
MELANIE:	You said you can buy a duck? I'm sure my children will both want one.	
ROB:	<u>They're on sale at a stall in the market</u>. You can't miss it – it's got an enormous sign showing a couple of ducks.	Q5
MELANIE:	OK. I'll go there this afternoon. I remember walking past there yesterday. Now could you tell me something about the flower show, please?	
ROB:	Well, admission is free, and the show is being held in <u>Bythwaite</u> Hall.	Q6
MELANIE:	Sorry, how do you spell that?	
ROB:	B-Y-T-H-W-A-I-T-E. Bythwaite.	
MELANIE:	Is it easy to find? I'm not very familiar with the town yet.	
ROB:	Oh, you won't have any problem. It's right in the centre of Stretton. It's the only old building in the town, so it's easy to recognise.	
MELANIE:	I know it. I presume it's open all day.	
ROB:	Yes, but if you'd like to see the prizes being awarded for the best flowers, you'll need to be there at 5 o'clock. <u>The prizes are being given by a famous actor, Kevin Shapless</u>. He lives nearby and gets involved in a lot of community events.	Q7
MELANIE:	Gosh, I've seen him on TV. I'll definitely go to the prize-giving.	
ROB:	Right.	

MELANIE:	I've seen a list of plays that are being performed this week, and I'd like to know which are suitable for my children, and which ones my husband and I might go to.	
ROB:	How old are your children?	
MELANIE:	Five and seven. What about 'The Mystery of Muldoon'?	
ROB:	<u>That's aimed at five to ten-year-olds</u>.	Q8
MELANIE:	So if I take my children, I can expect them to enjoy it more than I do?	
ROB:	I think so. <u>If you'd like something for yourself and your husband, and leave your children with a babysitter, you might like to see 'Fire and Flood'</u> – it's about events that really happened in Stretton two hundred years ago, and children might find it rather frightening.	Q9
MELANIE:	Oh, thanks for the warning. And finally, what about 'Silly Sailor'?	
ROB:	That's a comedy, and <u>it's for young and old</u>. In fact, it won an award in the Stretton Drama Festival a couple of months ago.	Q10
MELANIE:	OK. Well, goodbye, and thanks for all the information. I'm looking forward to the festival!	
ROB:	Goodbye.	

SECTION 2

Good morning, and welcome to the museum – one with a remarkable range of exhibits, which I'm sure you'll enjoy. My name's Greg, and I'll tell you about the various collections as we go round. But before we go, let me just give you a taste of what we have here.

Well, for one thing, we have a fine collection of twentieth and twenty-first century paintings, many by very well-known artists. I'm sure you'll recognise several of the paintings. <u>This is the gallery that attracts the largest number of visitors</u>, so it's best to go in early in the day, before the crowds arrive.   Q11

Then there are the nineteenth-century paintings. The museum was opened in the middle of that century, and <u>several of the artists each donated one work</u> – to get the museum started, as it were. So they're of special interest to us – we feel closer to them than to other works.   Q12

The sculpture gallery has a number of fine exhibits, but I'm afraid it's currently closed for refurbishment. You'll need to come back next year to see it properly, but <u>a number of the sculptures have been moved to other parts of the museum</u>.   Q13

<u>'Around the world' is a temporary exhibition – you've probably seen something about it on TV or in the newspapers</u>. It's created a great deal of interest, because it presents objects from every continent and many countries, and provides information about their social context – why they were made, who for, and so on.   Q14

Then there's the collection of coins. This is what you might call a focused, specialist collection, because all the coins come from this country, and were produced between two thousand and a thousand years ago. <u>And many of them were discovered by ordinary people digging their gardens, and donated to the museum!</u>   Q15

<u>All our porcelain and glass was left to the museum by its founder</u>, when he died in 1878. And in the terms of his will, we're not allowed to add anything to that collection: he believed it was perfect in itself, and we don't see any reason to disagree!   Q16

OK, that was something about the collections, and now here's some more practical information, in case you need it. Most of the museum facilities are downstairs, in the basement, so you go down the stairs here. When you reach the bottom of the stairs, you'll find yourself in a sitting area, with comfortable chairs and sofas where you can have a rest before continuing your exploration of the museum.

We have a very good restaurant, which serves excellent food all day, in a relaxing atmosphere. <u>To reach it, when you get to the bottom of the stairs, go straight ahead to the far side of the sitting area, then turn right into the corridor. You'll see the door of the restaurant facing you.</u>   Q17

If you just want a snack, or if you'd like to eat somewhere with facilities for children, we also have a café. <u>When you reach the bottom of the stairs, you'll need to go straight ahead, turn right into the corridor, and the café is immediately on the right</u>.   Q18

And talking about children, <u>there are baby-changing facilities downstairs: cross the sitting area, continue straight ahead along the corridor on the left, and you and your baby will find the facilities on the left-hand side</u>.   Q19

<u>The cloakroom, where you should leave coats, umbrellas and any large bags, is on the left hand side of the sitting area. It's through the last door before you come to the corridor</u>.   Q20

There are toilets on every floor, but in the basement they're the first rooms on the left when you get down there.

OK, now if you've got anything to leave in the cloakroom, please do that now, and then we'll start our tour.

SECTION 3

SUPERVISOR: Hi, Joanna, good to meet you. Now, before we discuss your new research project, I'd like to hear something about the psychology study you did last year for your Master's degree. So how did you choose your subjects for that?

JOANNA: Well, I had six subjects, all professional musicians, and all female. Three were violinists and there was also a cello player and a pianist and a flute player. They were all very highly regarded in the music world and <u>they'd done quite extensive tours in different continents</u>, and quite a few had won prizes and competitions as well.   Q21 & 22

SUPERVISOR:	And they were quite young, weren't they?	
JOANNA:	Yes, between 25 and 29 – the mean was 27.8. <u>I wasn't specifically looking for artists who'd produced recordings, but this is something that's just taken for granted these days, and they all had</u>.	Q21 & 22
SUPERVISOR:	Right. Now you collected your data through telephone interviews, didn't you?	
JOANNA:	Yes. <u>I realised if I was going to interview leading musicians it'd only be possible over the phone because they're so busy.</u> I recorded them using a telephone recording adaptor. I'd been worried about the quality, but it worked out all right. I managed at least a 30-minute interview with each subject, sometimes longer.	Q23 & 24
SUPERVISOR:	Did doing it on the phone make it more stressful?	
JOANNA:	I'd thought it might … it was all quite informal though and in fact they seemed very keen to talk. <u>And I don't think using the phone meant I got less rich data, rather the opposite in fact.</u>	Q23 & 24
SUPERVISOR:	Interesting. And you were looking at how performers dress for concert performances?	
JOANNA:	That's right. My research investigated the way players see their role as a musician and how this is linked to the type of clothing they decide to wear. But that focus didn't emerge immediately. <u>When I started I was more interested in trying to investigate the impact of what was worn on those listening</u>, and also <u>whether someone like a violinist might adopt a different style of clothing from, say, someone playing the flute or the trumpet.</u>	Q25 & 26 Q25 & 26
SUPERVISOR:	It's interesting that the choice of dress is up to the individual, isn't it?	
JOANNA:	Yes, you'd expect there to be rules about it in orchestras, but that's quite rare.	

SUPERVISOR:	You only had women performers in your study. Was that because male musicians are less worried about fashion?	
JOANNA:	I think a lot of the men are very much influenced by fashion, but <u>in social terms the choices they have are more limited … they'd really upset audiences if they strayed away from quite narrow boundaries</u>.	Q27
SUPERVISOR:	Hmm. Now, popular music has quite different expectations. Did you read Mike Frost's article about the dress of women performers in popular music?	
JOANNA:	No.	
SUPERVISOR:	He points out that a lot of female singers and musicians in popular music tend to dress down in performances, and wear less feminine clothes, like jeans instead of skirts, and <u>he suggests this is because otherwise they'd just be discounted as trivial</u>.	Q28
JOANNA:	But you could argue they're just wearing what's practical … I mean, a pop-music concert is usually a pretty energetic affair.	
SUPERVISOR:	Yes, he doesn't make that point, but I think you're probably right. I was interested by the effect of the audience at a musical performance when it came to the choice of dress.	
JOANNA:	The subjects I interviewed felt this was really important. It's all to do with what we understand by performance as a public event. <u>They believed the audience had certain expectations and it was up to them as performers to fulfil these expectations, to show a kind of esteem</u> …	Q29
SUPERVISOR:	… they weren't afraid of looking as if they'd made an effort to look good.	
JOANNA:	Mmm. I think in the past the audience would have had those expectations of one another too, but that's not really the case now, not in the UK anyway.	
SUPERVISOR:	No.	
JOANNA:	And I also got interested in what sports scientists are doing too, with regard to clothing.	

SUPERVISOR:	Musicians are quite vulnerable physically, aren't they, because the movements they carry out are very intensive and repetitive, so I'd imagine some features of sports clothing could safeguard the players from the potentially dangerous effects of this sort of thing.	*Q30*
JOANNA:	Yes, but musicians don't really consider it. They avoid clothing that obviously restricts their movements, but that's as far as they go.	
SUPERVISOR:	Anyway, coming back to your own research, do you have any idea where you're going from here?	
JOANNA:	I was thinking of doing a study using an audience, including …	

SECTION 4

As we saw in the last lecture, a major cause of climate change is the rapid rise in the level of carbon dioxide in the atmosphere over the last century. If we could reduce the amount of CO_2, perhaps the rate of climate change could also be slowed down. One potential method involves enhancing the role of the soil that plants grow in, with regard to absorbing CO_2. Rattan Lal, a soil scientist from Ohio State University, in the USA, claims that the world's agricultural soils could potentially absorb 13 per cent of the carbon dioxide in the atmosphere – the equivalent of the amount released in the last 30 years. And research is going on into how this might be achieved.

Lal first came to the idea that soil might be valuable in this way not through an interest in climate change, but rather out of concern for the land itself and the people dependent on it. Carbon-rich soil is dark, crumbly and fertile, and retains some water. But erosion can occur if soil is dry, which is a likely effect if it *Q31* contains inadequate amounts of carbon. Erosion is of course bad for people trying to grow crops or breed animals on that terrain. In the 1970s and '80s, Lal was studying soils in Africa so devoid of organic matter *Q32* that the ground had become extremely hard, like cement. There he met a pioneer in the study of global warming, who suggested that carbon from the soil had moved into the atmosphere. This is now looking increasingly likely.

Let me explain. For millions of years, carbon dioxide levels in the atmosphere have been regulated, in part, by a natural partnership between plants and microbes – tiny organisms in the soil. Plants absorb *Q33* CO_2 from the air and transform it into sugars and other carbon-based substances. While a proportion of these carbon products remain in the plant, some transfer from the roots to fungi and soil microbes, which *Q34* store the carbon in the soil.

The invention of agriculture some 10,000 years ago disrupted these ancient soil-building processes and led to the loss of carbon from the soil. When humans started draining the natural topsoil, and ploughing it up for planting, they exposed the buried carbon to oxygen. This created carbon dioxide and released it into the air. And in some places, grazing by domesticated animals has removed all vegetation, releasing carbon into the air. Tons of carbon have been stripped from the world's soils – where it's needed – and pumped into the atmosphere.

So what can be done? Researchers are now coming up with evidence that even modest changes to farming can significantly help to reduce the amount of carbon in the atmosphere.

Some growers have already started using an approach known as regenerative agriculture. This aims *Q35* to boost the fertility of soil and keep it moist through established practices. These include keeping fields planted all year round, and increasing the variety of plants being grown. Strategies like these can *Q36* significantly increase the amount of carbon stored in the soil, so agricultural researchers are now building a case for their use in combating climate change.

One American investigation into the potential for storing CO_2 on agricultural lands is taking place in California. Soil scientist Whendee Silver of the University of California, Berkeley, is conducting a first-of- *Q37* its-kind study on a large cattle farm in the state. She and her students are testing the effects on carbon storage of the compost that is created from waste – both agricultural, including manure and cornstalks, and <u>waste produced in gardens</u>, such as leaves, branches, and lawn trimmings.   *Q38*

In Australia, soil ecologist Christine Jones is testing another promising soil-enrichment strategy. Jones and 12 farmers are <u>working to build up soil carbon by cultivating grasses that stay green all year round</u>.   *Q39* Like composting, the approach has already been proved experimentally; Jones now hopes to show that it can be applied on working farms and that the resulting carbon capture can be accurately measured.

It's hoped in the future that projects such as these will demonstrate the role that farmers and other land managers can play in reducing the harmful effects of greenhouse gases. For example, in countries like the United States, where most farming operations use large applications of fertiliser, changing such long-standing habits will require a change of system. Rattan Lal argues that <u>farmers should receive payment</u>   *Q40* <u>not just for the corn or beef they produce, but also for the carbon they can store in their soil</u>.

Another study being carried out …

Listening and Reading Answer Keys

TEST 1

LISTENING

Section 1, Questions 1–10

1 Charlton
2 (£)115 / a/one hundred (and) fifteen
3 cash
4 parking
5 music
6 entry
7 stage
8 code
9 floor/floors
10 decoration/decorations

Section 2, Questions 11–20

11 animal/animals
12 tool/tools
13 shoes
14 dog/dogs
15 F
16 G
17 D
18 H
19 C
20 A

Section 3, Questions 21–30

21 C
22 B
23 B
24 C
25 A
26 B
27 C
28 A
29 B
30 A

Section 4, Questions 31–40

31 conservation
32 food/foods
33 surface
34 oxygen/O_2
35 mammals
36 ice
37 decline/declining/decrease
38 map
39 migration
40 consumption

If you score …

0–14	15–28	29–40
you are unlikely to get an acceptable score under examination conditions and we recommend that you spend a lot of time improving your English before you take IELTS.	you may get an acceptable score under examination conditions but we recommend that you think about having more practice or lessons before you take IELTS.	you are likely to get an acceptable score under examination conditions but remember that different institutions will find different scores acceptable.

READING

Section 1, Questions 1–14

1 TRUE
2 FALSE
3 NOT GIVEN
4 NOT GIVEN
5 NOT GIVEN
6 F
7 B
8 G
9 A
10 D
11 B
12 A
13 C
14 F

Section 2, Questions 15–27

15 marketing environment
16 Corporate Travel Consultant
17 rewards
18 outstanding efforts
19 ambitions
20 psychometric test
21 team
22 authorisation
23 obstructions
24 wrapped (carefully) / (carefully) wrapped
25 waste/rubbish
26 Trolleys
27 (regular) breaks

Section 3, Questions 28–40

28 vi
29 viii
30 iv
31 ii
32 ix
33 vii
34 x
35 harems
36 mares
37 herds
38 D
39 A
40 B

If you score …

0–20	21–31	32–40
you are unlikely to get an acceptable score under examination conditions and we recommend that you spend a lot of time improving your English before you take IELTS.	you may get an acceptable score under examination conditions but we recommend that you think about having more practice or lessons before you take IELTS.	you are likely to get an acceptable score under examination conditions but remember that different institutions will find different scores acceptable.

TEST 2

LISTENING

Section 1, Questions 1–10

1 hostel
2 Buckleigh
3 PE9 7QT
4 waiter
5 politics
6 cycling
7 cinema
8 disabled
9 4.30 (pm) / half past four
10 07788 136711

Section 2, Questions 11–20

11&12 *IN EITHER ORDER*
   A
   B
13&14 *IN EITHER ORDER*
   B
   D
15&16 *IN EITHER ORDER*
   C
   E
17 G
18 D
19 B
20 F

Section 3, Questions 21–30

21 A
22 A
23 C
24 B
25 B
26 B
27&28 *IN EITHER ORDER*
   A
   D
29&30 *IN EITHER ORDER*
   C
   E

Section 4, Questions 31–40

31 social
32 factory
33 canal
34 bridge
35 box
36 screen
37 rubber
38 curved
39 curtains
40 international

If you score …

0–14	15–28	29–40
you are unlikely to get an acceptable score under examination conditions and we recommend that you spend a lot of time improving your English before you take IELTS.	you may get an acceptable score under examination conditions but we recommend that you think about having more practice or lessons before you take IELTS.	you are likely to get an acceptable score under examination conditions but remember that different institutions will find different scores acceptable.

READING

Section 1, Questions 1–14

1 NOT GIVEN
2 FALSE
3 TRUE
4 FALSE
5 TRUE
6 NOT GIVEN
7 D
8 E
9 I
10 F
11 H
12 D
13 G
14 C

Section 3, Questions 28–40

28 viii
29 ii
30 x
31 iv
32 vii
33 v
34 iii
35 vi
36 FALSE
37 TRUE
38 NOT GIVEN
39 FALSE
40 NOT GIVEN

Section 2, Questions 15–27

15 colleague
16 power cut
17 breathing
18 displacement activity
19 conversation
20 reactions
21 examples
22 handouts
23 internships
24 skills
25 cuttings
26 research
27 errors

If you score …

0–20	21–31	32–40
you are unlikely to get an acceptable score under examination conditions and we recommend that you spend a lot of time improving your English before you take IELTS.	you may get an acceptable score under examination conditions but we recommend that you think about having more practice or lessons before you take IELTS.	you are likely to get an acceptable score under examination conditions but remember that different institutions will find different scores acceptable.

TEST 3

LISTENING

Section 1, Questions 1–10

1	B
2	C
3	B
4	A
5	C
6	A
7	birds
8	flowers
9	mushrooms
10	river

Section 2, Questions 11–20

11	C
12	B
13	B
14	A
15	C
16	G
17	A
18	C
19	B
20	F

Section 3, Questions 21–30

21	cave
22	tiger
23	dancing
24	crying
25	grass
26	scarf
27	A
28	C
29	D
30	B

Section 4, Questions 31–40

31	attitude/attitudes
32	numbers
33	time/minutes
34	software
35	patients
36	emotions/feelings
37	income
38	comfortable
39	observation
40	analysis

If you score …

0–14	15–30	31–40
you are unlikely to get an acceptable score under examination conditions and we recommend that you spend a lot of time improving your English before you take IELTS.	you may get an acceptable score under examination conditions but we recommend that you think about having more practice or lessons before you take IELTS.	you are likely to get an acceptable score under examination conditions but remember that different institutions will find different scores acceptable.

READING

Section 1, Questions 1–14

1	F
2	H
3	E
4	G
5	D
6	C
7	NOT GIVEN
8	TRUE
9	FALSE
10	FALSE
11	TRUE
12	FALSE
13	NOT GIVEN
14	TRUE

Section 3, Questions 28–40

28	vii
29	iv
30	ii
31	vi
32	iii
33	viii
34	B
35	D
36	C
37	A
38	tundra
39	insects
40	predators

Section 2, Questions 15–27

15	holiday
16	breakout
17	notice
18	summary
19	badge
20	questionnaires
21	promotion
22	questions
23	responsibilities
24	calmly
25	goals
26	progress
27	dedication

If you score …

0–18	19–29	30–40
you are unlikely to get an acceptable score under examination conditions and we recommend that you spend a lot of time improving your English before you take IELTS.	you may get an acceptable score under examination conditions but we recommend that you think about having more practice or lessons before you take IELTS.	you are likely to get an acceptable score under examination conditions but remember that different institutions will find different scores acceptable.

TEST 4

LISTENING

Section 1, Questions 1–10

1	secondary
2	flute
3	cinema
4	concert
5	market
6	Bythwaite
7	actor
8	A
9	B
10	C

Section 2, Questions 11–20

11	E
12	D
13	G
14	B
15	C
16	A
17	F
18	H
19	C
20	B

Section 3, Questions 21–30

21&22	*IN EITHER ORDER*
	B
	D
23&24	*IN EITHER ORDER*
	A
	B
25&26	*IN EITHER ORDER*
	B
	E
27	C
28	A
29	A
30	C

Section 4, Questions 31–40

31	dry
32	hard
33	sugar/sugars
34	roots
35	moist/damp/wet
36	variety
37	cattle
38	gardens/gardening
39	grasses
40	payment/payments / money

If you score …

0–14	15–28	29–40
you are unlikely to get an acceptable score under examination conditions and we recommend that you spend a lot of time improving your English before you take IELTS.	you may get an acceptable score under examination conditions but we recommend that you think about having more practice or lessons before you take IELTS.	you are likely to get an acceptable score under examination conditions but remember that different institutions will find different scores acceptable.

READING

Section 1, Questions 1–14

1 E
2 B
3 F
4 B
5 A
6 C
7 A
8 TRUE
9 FALSE
10 NOT GIVEN
11 TRUE
12 FALSE
13 FALSE
14 TRUE

Section 2, Questions 15–27

15 confidence
16 website
17 duties
18 charity
19 ambitions
20 gaps
21 salary
22 competitors
23 delivery
24 premises
25 law
26 costs
27 funding

Section 3, Questions 28–40

28 v
29 ix
30 iii
31 vii
32 ii
33 viii
34 C
35 A
36 C
37 stamina/energy
38 dog
39 vision
40 ears

If you score …

0–20	21–31	32–40
you are unlikely to get an acceptable score under examination conditions and we recommend that you spend a lot of time improving your English before you take IELTS.	you may get an acceptable score under examination conditions but we recommend that you think about having more practice or lessons before you take IELTS.	you are likely to get an acceptable score under examination conditions but remember that different institutions will find different scores acceptable.

Sample answers for Writing tasks

TEST 1, WRITING TASK 1

SAMPLE ANSWER

This is an answer written by a candidate who achieved a **Band 7** score. Here is the examiner's comment:

> The response is relevant and appropriate. The candidate presents each bullet point clearly and extends/supports each one well. Ideas are logically organised and there is clear progression throughout the response. Use of discourse markers is managed somewhat mechanically (*At first, However, Next, also, Lastly, as well, In conclusion*), but there is good use of other cohesive devices such as reference and substitution, although there are some instances of inaccuracy (*it, such a people, the reason why this happen, For that reason, most valuable point, them, for these reason*). The range of lexis demonstrates some flexibility and precision, as well as an awareness of style and collocation (*disadvantage, around same age as you, just have fun with friends, very difficult to enter Japanese colleges, graduate, huge, not cheap, waste of money, reception, collegue/colleague, customers, English skill*), although occasional errors in spelling and word formation occur. A variety of complex structures is attempted, but the grammatical control is variable: this lack of control is probably the weakest aspect of this script.

Dear Haruka.

Hello Haruka. I am writing a reply to your letter that asking for advice about whether to go to college or to try to get a job. I thing trying to get a job is better for you. I would like to write reasons why.

At first, I will mention about disadvantage of going to college. I think you would not enjoy it, because in a college, especially Japanese college, you could only meet people who are around same age as you. You must have already met such a people in your junior high school and high school. In addition to it, many students tend to just have fun with friends beside study. The reason why this happen, it is usually very difficult to enter Japanese colleges but to graduate it is not so difficult. for that reason, many students tend to just have enjoy, like having parties, going out, going travel. However college costs a huge of money on you. The fee of it is not cheap of course. I think it is waste of money to go to college.

Next, I would tell you why getting a job is good idea for you. The most valuable point is experience. Not like college, you can see many people from different age of you. By talking with them, you can get many knowledge of life and it would be good for you. Not only from people, you can also get important experience from working. You could know how different to earn the money and also you can know many social system as well.

Lastly I would like to suggest the types of job that would be suitable for you. I think you good at talking with people, so the reception of company, school or hotel would be good. You can meet not only collegue but also many people of customers. If you would get a job of hotel, you can use your English skill as well.

In conclusion, I should try to get a job for these reason. Good luck for you

TEST 1, WRITING TASK 2

SAMPLE ANSWER

This is an answer written by a candidate who achieved a **Band 6** score. Here is the examiner's comment:

> The candidate addresses all parts of the prompt appropriately, with examples or extension to illustrate and support his ideas. His own position is clearly stated in the third part of the response. His response to the task is the best aspect of the script, but further support and extension would be required to achieve a higher band here. There is a clear overall progression in the response; discourse markers are used somewhat mechanically, with occasional errors (*Sometimes, For instance, In the other hand, Firstly, Secondly, In my opinion, At final*) and there are some attempts to use other cohesive devices (*In this case*), but paragraphing is poorly handled, with some 'paragraphs' consisting of a single sentence. The lexical resource is both adequate and appropriate for the task, showing some awareness of style and collocation (*family situation, confidential, suburb of Paris, curriculum vitae, position, skills and degrees, discrimination, united, share the same interests and hobbies, good relationships between each member, a balanced life*), but there are also errors in word formation and spelling (*job's candidats, impopular, work's team, wich, request/require, familial*), as well as two instances where meaning is unclear (*rentability, performant*). There is a mix of simple and complex sentence forms, but there are errors in grammatical control, e.g. (*This people hadn't been choose for the position, some employers prefers, a man … who have*).

Sometimes, in interviews, some employers ask job's candidats for personnal information such as hobbies and interests, or family situation.

Some people think that this information should be confidential and candidats for jobs don't have to give private information to employers.

For instance, in a suburb of Paris, people applying for jobs said, in their Curriculum Vitae, they lived in a very impopular suburb and they practiced Rap Music. This people hadn't been choose for the position while they had all the skills and degrees for it.

In this case, personal information can be the cause of a kind of "discriminations"

In the other hand, some employers prefers to have very united work's team because they think it's a factor to improve rentability in companies. In this case, personal information such as hobbies and interests could be very precious.

Finally, a work's team who share the same interests and hobbies is more performant because of the good relationships between each member.

Secondly, a man applying for jobs, who have hobbies and interests, shows that he have a balanced life. It's the same for a woman.

In my opinion, give some personnal information when I have an interview for a job could be a way of talking about me. I think an employer have to know wich person he has in front of him. It's much more important if the position request responsibility.

At final, even so sometimes it's not really relevant or useful to give personal information for people applying for job, most of employers have to know their interests, hobbies, or familial situation.

TEST 2, WRITING TASK 1

SAMPLE ANSWER

This is an answer written by a candidate who achieved a **Band 4.5** score. Here is the examiner's comment:

> The candidate has written to the hotel manager as required, but the three bullet points are not covered adequately. It is not clear where the writer thinks he or she has left the papers (only that they are somewhere in the hotel), nor is it clear what he or she wants the manager to do with them when found. There are also problems with the tone and format of the letter. Information and ideas are presented, but these are not arranged coherently and there are few cohesive devices. The range of vocabulary is limited, but just adequate for the task, with some errors in word choice and formation (*I conference your hotel, total 280paper, a level of doctor*). The range of grammatical structures is limited and although there are a few attempts at subordination (*I hope you to remember that …, I'll using the report when, I belive you already have it when, When you finished reading it, when I finised the presentation*), they are almost all 'when' clauses. The level of error is high, even in simple structures (*The date is start, I have no enough time, I really want finding*) and punctuation is also often faulty.

Dear Sir. Hello. I have a request to your hotel. I have been there and I hope you to remember that I conference your hotel few days ago.

My name is --- and room No. is 707. The date. is start 12/02/14 to 17/02/14. Actually, I lost my report for presentation. That is total 280paper. It was specially requested to Japan Uni for 1 month. I'll using the report when I get a level of doctor.

I have no enough time for collected report again. Because the presentation will be opened after 4 days. I really want finding the report, and I belive you already have it when you before reading this mail.

Protect the lost goods is due the hotels.

And already it's a law.

When you finished reading it, then just call me or leave your message to my asistant. I have a plan that when I finised the presentation, I'll be go there again for celerbrat party with my friends.

Generally,

----.

TEST 2, WRITING TASK 2

SAMPLE ANSWER

This is an answer written by a candidate who achieved a **Band 6.5** score. Here is the examiner's comment:

> The candidate addresses all parts of the task and presents a clear position throughout the response. Ideas are presented, extended and supported, arranged coherently and there is a clear overall progression. Cohesive devices are used effectively, but paragraphing is not adequate – many of the 'paragraphs' consist of a single sentence. The range of vocabulary is sufficient to allow some flexibility and precision, and shows an awareness of style and collocation (*reflection, research, balanced in terms of theory and …, personal and professional problems*). There is a variety of complex structures with frequent error-free sentences and good control over grammar and punctuation.

I agree with people who say that too much time is spent on learning facts and not enough on learning practical skills, in all levels of educations.

Since I was child, I've been studying in different sorts of institution and I could realize – mainly when I started to work – that most of the time we spend more time in 'what' or 'why' do something than 'how' do it.

For sure I believe it's important to know the theory through what 'things works'. This knowledge encourage the reflection, the research, and so on …

That's why the education standard is: in one side there is a teacher explaining the subject and in another side there are the students trying to learn everything.

Usually, there are few practical classes, when we can really develop our skills, for example: laboratory classes and computer classes.

Even in my university course – Industrial Engineering – there are few practical tasks.

That's why I think the structure of education could be more balanced in terms of theory and practical skills. I this way people would be more capable to cope with personal and professional problems.

I believe that some institutions have already realized the importance of this balanced education. Some evidences to prove it: the increasing number of study cases and tasks which involve real problems like solving a marketing problem in a real company. Other evidence is the increasing number of MBAs offered around the world.

Therefore, I agree that we need to promote more the practical skills, but, as I see it, this change has been occuring

TEST 3, WRITING TASK 1

SAMPLE ANSWER

This is an answer written by a candidate who achieved a **Band 7** score. Here is the examiner's comment:

> The candidate states the purpose of the letter at the outset. All three bullet points are covered and clearly highlighted (even though the first and second bullet points are addressed in reverse order). Information and ideas are logically organised and there is a clear progression throughout the response. There is some flexibility and precision in the use of lexis and evidence of ability to use less common items (*underestimate the importance of this center, the influence of sporting activities … on the health of the people, fitness lessons for adults, negative concequences, the opportunity to spend their time in a healthy atmosphere*). US spelling is used consistently throughout; spelling and word choice errors are only occasional (*meat/meet, concequences the closure of the center could do*). There is a variety of complex structures, used with some flexibility and accuracy (*raise my concern regarding …, provided it doesn't rain, people could become less engaged in … affect their health, for the people interested in sport it will become more difficult to …*). There are a few grammatical errors, but these do not impede communication.

Dear Sir or Madam,

My name is Irana Smirnova and I am writing to raise my concern regarding the plans to close our local sports and leisure center. It is hard to underestimate the importance of this center for citizens; in fact, it became the point where we all meat each other to share some positive emotions and spend free time. Also, one cannot miss the influence of sporting activities provided there on the health of the people.

My family is used to going to the center several times a week. My husband and I attend fitness lessons for adults on Monday and Wednesday after work. My two sons went to the center after school; they have a place there to do their homework., to play with other children and relax in safe environment. On weekends we usually meet friends there and go to the swimming pool ore open-air tennis courts provided it doesn't rain cats and dogs.

I can think of several negative concequences the closure of the center could do. Firstly, people could become less engaged in sport activities which will definitely affect their health. Secondly, children will lose the opportunity to spend their time in a healthy atmosphere and will spend more time at the street. Finally, for the people interested in sport it will become more difficult to get to the place to exercize as the nearest sports center in in Tornton which is 30 miles away.

I believe this question deserves close attention.

Yours faithfully

Irina Smirnova

TEST 3, WRITING TASK 2

SAMPLE ANSWER

This is an answer written by a candidate who achieved a **Band 6** score. Here is the examiner's comment:

> All parts of the prompt are addressed and a position is presented that is directly relevant to the prompt. Main ideas are relevant, but some would benefit from further development. Ideas are generally arranged coherently and there is a clear overall progression. Some paragraphs are rather short, due to a lack of development of ideas. The range of lexis is generally adequate and appropriate for the task, with only a few spelling errors. There is a mix of simple and complex sentence structures, generally produced accurately.

In our daily life, we see many photos or images of news events in newspapers and on television. Some people say that the images are more effective to tell the truth than words. Basically I agree to this idea, but there are some different idea as well.

The idea that showing pictures is the effective way is obviously true, because we can see a lot of photos and images in media. We can see the atmosphere, facial expressions and background sceneries from the photos. Everybody believes that watching is more important than hearing.

In addition, young people do not like reading recently. They are used to collecting information from the internet rather than books. For the young generation, images should be much more effective than reading every single letters, needless to say.

However, photos cannot tell more than they show. You can see a facial expression of a murderer in the picture, but you never know his history or habits without reading an investigation about him. When the East Japan Earthquake occurred, I read a lot of newspaper articles about the families of victims. There are a huge amount of stories of children who lost parents with Tsunami and a man who lost his wife with a baby in her tummy, and so on. At that time, I felt strongly that words are much more effective that pictures.

To sum up, if I am asked the question which more effective is, pictures or words, I would say pictures. But we should be more flexible to accept reading words as well as watching images, not escaping from letters. We have to try to collect the balanced information from media, not only by the pictures, but also valuable words.

TEST 4, WRITING TASK 1

SAMPLE ANSWER

This is an answer written by a candidate who achieved a **Band 5** score. Here is the examiner's comment:

> The response generally addresses the task and the purpose is generally clear. However, the tone is not always appropriate (*I want the company to pay for my course …, Please I ask you, will you pay for my course …*). The bullet points are covered but there is quite a lot of repetition. There is information about the course (*The course shows how to use internet, use software and other usefull thing about computers …*) but there could be more detail. The information is quite well organised and the paragraphs are clear, but there needs to be more referencing and substitution (*computer, company, my job, course*). Some basic cohesive devices are used (*and, so, if, this, it*), but there need to be more linking devices, e.g. in the third paragraph. There is some good vocabulary (*benefit, uses software*), but it is rather limited, and there are some spelling errors (*usefull*). The range of structures is limited and there are errors in complex sentences (*If company pay, it is good for company and good for my work …, I can't afford to pay for course so I hope you can helping me with this*). Some simple sentences are accurate (*I know you will not regret it …*), but there are a lot of grammar errors, e.g. articles (*the, a*).

Dear Sir/Madam,

I am write for apply training course which I see in advertisment. The training course is for computers and it can helping me for my job. I need to learn more about use computer and this course can be usefull for me. I need to use computer a lot, so I will benefit from this and the company will also benefit because I will be good at using it for my job. The course shows how to use internet, use software and other usefull thing about computers.

I want the company to pay for my course. If company pay, it is good for company and good for my work. I can't afford to pay for course so I hope you can helping me with this.

Please I ask you, will you pay for my course. I know you will not regret it. You will see I am very good at use computers in my job.

TEST 4, WRITING TASK 2

MODEL ANSWER

This is an answer written by a candidate who achieved a **Band 7** score. Here is the examiner's comment:

> The response addresses all parts of the task and there is a clear opinion. Ideas are usually expressed fully, but they sometimes need more support. Organisation is logical and there is a clear central topic to each paragraph. There is a good range of cohesive devices, although there are some errors (*As character is concerned …, There are some people which …*). Substitution is usually good, although there is some repetition (*basic things*) in the first paragraph. There is a good range of vocabulary and there are some less common words and phrases (*distinctive, ethnic origins, Another aspect of dress is, grubby, misleading, they are not just following fashion …*). There are some word choice errors (*national style of wear*), and spelling errors (*nowdays, personalitys*). There is a good range of complex structures and many sentences have accurate grammar and punctuation. There are a few errors in grammar (*how much concerned they about to be smart*).

It is certainly a very interesting question. Does what a person wears tell us so much about their culture and personality or not? I tend to agree that clothes can tell us some basic things, but that they do not tell us much more than those basic things.

First of all, I will consider how a person's choice of clothes reveals their culture. This is true in some ways, for example, in many countries people have a distinctive national style of wear, and some particular cloths and fabrics are typical of certain areas. Therefore, clothes can sometimes reveal the ethnic origins and culture of a person, but as so many people nowdays dress in business suits or jeans and T-shirts worldwide this is becoming less and less true.

As character is concerned, we can tell in some places if the wearer of clothes is a follower of fashion. Another aspect of dress is whether the clothes look clean and ironed or grubby and very casual. This might tell us how much concerned they are about to be smart. However, the way someone dresses can also be misleading at times. There are some people which wears clothes that seems very unusual and strange but often they are just following fashion and are not unusual or strange people in their personalitys at all.

To sum up, I would say that we can find out something about a person from their style of dress but only the surface things, and not the deeper character.

Sample answer sheets

BRITISH COUNCIL

idp IELTS AUSTRALIA

CAMBRIDGE ENGLISH Language Assessment
Part of the University of Cambridge

IELTS Listening and Reading Answer Sheet

Centre number:

Pencil must be used to complete this sheet.

Please write your **full name** in CAPITAL letters on the line below:

SAMPLE

Then write your six digit Candidate number in the boxes and shade the number in the grid on the right.

0 1 2 3 4 5 6 7 8 9

Test date (shade ONE box for the day, ONE box for the month and ONE box for the year):

Day: 01 02 03 04 05 06 07 08 09 10 11 12 13 14 15 16 17 18 19 20 21 22 23 24 25 26 27 28 29 30 31

Month: 01 02 03 04 05 06 07 08 09 10 11 12   Year (last 2 digits): 13 14 15 16 17 18 19 20 21

	Listening		Marker use only		Listening		Marker use only
1			✓ 1 ✗	21			✓ 21 ✗
2			✓ 2 ✗	22			✓ 22 ✗
3			✓ 3 ✗	23			✓ 23 ✗
4			✓ 4 ✗	24			✓ 24 ✗
5			✓ 5 ✗	25			✓ 25 ✗
6			✓ 6 ✗	26			✓ 26 ✗
7			✓ 7 ✗	27			✓ 27 ✗
8			✓ 8 ✗	28			✓ 28 ✗
9			✓ 9 ✗	29			✓ 29 ✗
10			✓ 10 ✗	30			✓ 30 ✗
11			✓ 11 ✗	31			✓ 31 ✗
12			✓ 12 ✗	32			✓ 32 ✗
13			✓ 13 ✗	33			✓ 33 ✗
14			✓ 14 ✗	34			✓ 34 ✗
15			✓ 15 ✗	35			✓ 35 ✗
16			✓ 16 ✗	36			✓ 36 ✗
17			✓ 17 ✗	37			✓ 37 ✗
18			✓ 18 ✗	38			✓ 38 ✗
19			✓ 19 ✗	39			✓ 39 ✗
20			✓ 20 ✗	40			✓ 40 ✗

Marker 2 Signature   Marker 1 Signature   Listening Total

IELTS L-R v1.0   **denote** Print Limited 0121 520 5100   DP787/394

Sample answer sheets

Please write your **full name** in CAPITAL letters on the line below:

SAMPLE

Please write your Candidate number on the line below:

_____

Please write your three digit language code
in the boxes and shade the numbers in the
grid on the right.

0 1 2 3 4 5 6 7 8 9
0 1 2 3 4 5 6 7 8 9
0 1 2 3 4 5 6 7 8 9

Are you: Female? ▭ Male? ▭

Reading Reading Reading Reading Reading Reading

Module taken (shade one box): Academic ▭ General Training ▭

	Marker use only
1	✓ 1 ✗
2	✓ 2 ✗
3	✓ 3 ✗
4	✓ 4 ✗
5	✓ 5 ✗
6	✓ 6 ✗
7	✓ 7 ✗
8	✓ 8 ✗
9	✓ 9 ✗
10	✓ 10 ✗
11	✓ 11 ✗
12	✓ 12 ✗
13	✓ 13 ✗
14	✓ 14 ✗
15	✓ 15 ✗
16	✓ 16 ✗
17	✓ 17 ✗
18	✓ 18 ✗
19	✓ 19 ✗
20	✓ 20 ✗

	Marker use only
21	✓ 21 ✗
22	✓ 22 ✗
23	✓ 23 ✗
24	✓ 24 ✗
25	✓ 25 ✗
26	✓ 26 ✗
27	✓ 27 ✗
28	✓ 28 ✗
29	✓ 29 ✗
30	✓ 30 ✗
31	✓ 31 ✗
32	✓ 32 ✗
33	✓ 33 ✗
34	✓ 34 ✗
35	✓ 35 ✗
36	✓ 36 ✗
37	✓ 37 ✗
38	✓ 38 ✗
39	✓ 39 ✗
40	✓ 40 ✗

Marker 2 Signature		Marker 1 Signature		Reading Total	

BRITISH COUNCIL **idp** IELTS AUSTRALIA **CAMBRIDGE ENGLISH** Language Assessment Part of the University of Cambridge

IELTS Writing Answer Sheet – TASK 1

Candidate Name

Centre Number

Candidate Number

Module (shade one box):   Academic ☐   General Training ☐

Test date

D D   M M   Y Y Y Y

TASK 1

Do not write below this line

100913/2

BRITISH COUNCIL · **idp** IELTS AUSTRALIA · **CAMBRIDGE ENGLISH** Language Assessment Part of the University of Cambridge

IELTS Writing Answer Sheet – TASK 2

Candidate Name

Centre Number

Candidate Number

Module (shade one box):   Academic ☐   General Training ☐

Test date

D D   M M   Y Y Y Y

TASK 2

Do not write below this line

100895/2

Acknowledgements

The authors and publishers acknowledge the following sources of copyright material and are grateful for the permissions granted. While every effort has been made, it has not always been possible to identify the sources of all the material used, or to trace all copyright holders. If any omissions are brought to our notice, we will be happy to include the appropriate acknowledgements on reprinting and in the next update to the digital edition, as applicable.

Text on pp. 18–19 adapted from 'School Attendance: Information for Parents/Carers' January 2008, Cambs County Council with permission;

Text on pp. 28–29 adapted from 'March of the zebras' by James Gifford, *BBC Wildlife Autumn 2011*, Vol 29, No 10. Text adapted from original article by James Gifford, published in *BBC Wildlife* magazine © Immediate Media Company Ltd;

Text on p. 41 adapted from 'Sustainable school travel strategy' leaflet, Cambs County Council with permission;

Text on p. 43 adapted from 'Stop flu before it stops you' leaflet, novartis.co.uk, Novartis Vaccines and Diagnostics Limited. Reproduced with permission;

Text on p. 45 adapted from 'Tips for giving an effective business presentation', www.impactfactory.com. Reproduced with permission;

Text on pp. 50–51 adapted from 'A working life: The supermarket manager' by Jill Insley, The Guardian, 08.07.2011 © Guardian News and Media Limited 2011.

Text on p. 63 adapted from 'Summer at Kew 2010' leaflet, Royal Botanic Gardens. Reproduced with permission;

Text on p. 65 adapted from 'Norwich Park and Ride', Norfolk County Council. Reproduced with permission;

Text on p. 67 adapted from 'How to arrange and run a conference', British Association for Sexual Health and HIV (BASHH). Reproduced with permission;

Text on p. 69 adapted from 'How to Write the Best Employee Performance Appraisals' by Barb Nefer, Livestrong.com, 27.01.15. Copyright © Demand Media, Inc.;

Text on pp. 72–73 adapted from 'Saving a sandpiper' by Gerrit Vyn, BBC Wildlife Magazine, October 2012. Copyright © Immediate Media Company Ltd;

Text on p. 88 adapted from 'Learning to Paraglide', Hang Gliding Federation of Australia. Reproduced with permission;

Text on p. 90 adapted from 'Preparing for an interview' by Melanie Allen, May 2008. Copyright © jobs.ac.uk;

Text on p. 92 adapted from 'Setting up a Business', http://www.netmums.com/back-to-work/working-for-yourself/setting-up-a-business. Reproduced with permission of Netmums Ltd.